COLLECTIONS

A Harcourt Reading / Language Arts Program

JOURNEYS OF WONDER

TEACHER'S EDITION

SENIOR AUTHORS

Roger C. Farr • Dorothy S. Strickland • Isabel L. Beck

AUTHORS

Richard F. Abrahamson • Alma Flor Ada • Bernice E. Cullinan • Margaret McKeown • Nancy Roser
Patricia Smith • Judy Wallis • Junko Yokota • Hallie Kay Yopp

SENIOR CONSULTANT

Asa G. Hilliard III

CONSULTANTS

Karen S. Kutiper • David A. Monti • Angelina Olivares

Harcourt

Orlando Boston Dallas Chicago San Diego

Visit *The Learning Site!*
www.harcourtschool.com

Acknowledgments appear in the back of this book.

Printed in the United States of America

ISBN 0-15-318925-8

4 5 6 7 8 9 10 030 2002 2001

Meet Our Authors!

Senior Authors

Dr. Roger C. Farr
Chancellor's Professor and Director of the Center for Innovation in Assessment, Indiana University, Bloomington

RESEARCH CONTRIBUTIONS: Assessment, Portfolios, Reading-Writing Strategies, Staff Development

Dr. Dorothy S. Strickland
The State of New Jersey Professor of Reading, Rutgers University

RESEARCH CONTRIBUTIONS: Emergent Literacy, Linguistic and Cultural Diversity, Intervention, Phonics in Literature-based Curriculum, Integrated Language Arts, Assessment

Dr. Isabel L. Beck
Professor of Education and Senior Scientist at the Learning Research and Development Center, University of Pittsburgh

RESEARCH CONTRIBUTIONS: Beginning Reading, Reading Comprehension, Vocabulary, Phonics/Decoding Instruction, Critical Thinking, Technology

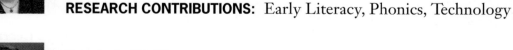

Authors

Dr. Richard F. Abrahamson
Professor of Education, University of Houston
RESEARCH CONTRIBUTIONS: Children's Literature, Strategic Reading, Reading Nonfiction

Dr. Alma Flor Ada
Director of Doctoral Studies in the International Multicultural Program, University of San Francisco
RESEARCH CONTRIBUTIONS: Bilingual Education, English as a Second Language, Family Involvement

Dr. Bernice E. Cullinan
Professor of Early Childhood and Elementary Education, New York University
RESEARCH CONTRIBUTIONS: Children's Literature, Emergent Literacy, Intervention, Integrated Language Arts

Dr. Margaret McKeown
Research Scientist at the Learning and Development Center, University of Pittsburgh
RESEARCH CONTRIBUTIONS: Reading Comprehension, Vocabulary

Dr. Nancy Roser
Professor, Language and Literacy Studies, University of Texas, Austin
RESEARCH CONTRIBUTIONS: Beginning Reading, Book Discussions, Early Childhood, Emergent Literacy, Phonics in Literature-based Curriculum, Reading Comprehension

Patricia Smith
Elementary Reading/Language Arts Coordinator, Cypress-Fairbanks School District, Houston, Texas, and Adjunct Professor of Education, University of Houston-Clear Lake
RESEARCH CONTRIBUTIONS: Early Literacy, Phonics, Technology

Dr. Judy Wallis
Coordinator for Elementary Arts and Social Studies, Alief Independent School District, Houston, Texas
RESEARCH CONTRIBUTIONS: Integrated Language Arts, Reading Strategies

Dr. Junko Yokota
Associate Professor, Reading/Language Arts Department, National-Louis University, Evanston, Illinois
RESEARCH CONTRIBUTIONS: Multicultural Literature, Children's Literature

Dr. Hallie Kay Yopp
Professor, Department of Elementary Bilingual and Reading Education, California State University, Fullerton
RESEARCH CONTRIBUTIONS: Phonemic Awareness, Early Childhood

Senior Consultant

Dr. Asa G. Hilliard III
Fuller E. Callaway Professor of Urban Education, Department of Educational Foundations, Georgia State University, Atlanta
RESEARCH CONTRIBUTIONS: Multicultural Literature and Education

Consultants

Dr. Karen S. Kutiper
English/Language Arts Consultant, Harris County Department of Education, Texas
RESEARCH CONTRIBUTIONS: Early Literacy, Reader Response

Dr. David A. Monti
Professor, Reading/Language Arts Department, Central Connecticut State University
RESEARCH CONTRIBUTIONS: Flexible Grouping, Technology, Family Involvement

Angelina Olivares
Elementary Coordinator, Bilingual/ESL, Fort Worth Independent School District
RESEARCH CONTRIBUTIONS: Spanish Reading, English as a Second Language, Bilingual Education

Program Features

***Collections** is a balanced, comprehensive program that provides the materials and support you need to help all your students become fluent, lifelong readers.*

*The foundation of **Collections** is research-based instruction and practice, organized in practical, easy-to-use lessons and components.*

*You will find the following features of effective reading instruction throughout the **Collections** program.*

Literature

- **Wide reading** in a variety of **classic** and **contemporary works,** including realistic fiction, folktales, informational nonfiction, biography and autobiography, plays, and poems.
- Accessible, appropriate literature for **instructional-level reading.**
- Opportunities to self-select **trade books** for independent, sustained reading.
- Instruction in **setting purposes** for reading, **monitoring comprehension,** and using **reading strategies.**
- Instruction in distinguishing among different **genres** and **types of text.**
- Opportunities to **respond to literature** in ways that demonstrate comprehension, interpretation, and appreciation.

Where to Find It

- Hidden Surprises and Journeys of Wonder Student Editions
- New Adventures Intervention Reader
- Reader's Choice Library
- Leveled Library
- Multi-Level Books
- Monitor Comprehension and Guided Reading

Oral Language

- Frequent listening opportunities to **develop vocabulary** and promote a **love of literature.**
- Lively discussions that focus on **interpreting** literature, **connecting** ideas and experiences, and **solving problems.**
- Oral reading and **retelling** activities, with assessment suggestions.
- Oral rereading to build **fluency** and **automatic word recognition.**
- Listening and speaking activities to help students **listen responsively** and **speak with expression,** appropriate volume and rate, and attention to phrasing and punctuation.

Where to Find It

- Listening to Literature
- *Read-Aloud Anthology*
- Literature Cassettes
- Building Background and Concepts
- Building Literacy Skills

Word Identification

- **Decoding instruction,** appropriately sequenced and maintained through the grades.
- Direct instruction in using **letter-sound correspondences, structural cues,** and common **syllable patterns.**
- Opportunities to **apply decoding skills** during reading.
- Abundant **review and practice** activities.
- Multiple opportunities to read and reread, building **accuracy** and **fluency.**

Where to Find It

- Build Word-Identification Strategies
- Reviewing Word-Identification Strategies
- Decoding/Phonics skill lessons
- Decoding Long Words and Word Study activities
- Phonics Express™ CD-ROM
- Phonics Practice Book
- Phonics Practice Readers

Program Features

Vocabulary

- Direct instruction in word **meanings** and **usage.**
- Systematic vocabulary **introduction, review,** and **practice.**
- Strategies for confirming meaning and pronunciation through **syntax, context, references,** and **resources.**
- Instruction in word parts such as **prefixes, suffixes,** and **root words.**
- Engaging activities and lessons, using **synonyms, antonyms, homophones, homographs, specialized vocabulary,** and **cross-curricular words.**
- Ongoing vocabulary development through **extensive reading** and **listening.**

Where to Find It

- Introducing Vocabulary
- Reviewing Vocabulary Words
- Extending Vocabulary
- Vocabulary Skill Lessons
- Develop Vocabulary Through Listening

Comprehension

- Carefully organized instructional plan that includes **preteaching** the skill before reading, **applying** the skill during reading, and **reinforcing** and **practicing** the skill after reading.
- **Systematic instruction** that builds through the grades, with each tested skill introduced, retaught, reviewed at least twice, and maintained after testing and in subsequent grades as appropriate.
- Ongoing **strategy development** to help students gain meaning from text and build independence.
- Questions and activities to build **critical-thinking** skills.
- Retelling and **summarizing** activities to assess comprehension.
- **Test preparation** to equip students for success on standardized and state tests.

Where to Find It

- Skill lessons in both the *Teacher's Edition* and *Student Edition*
- Using Reading Strategies and Strategy Reminders
- Monitor Comprehension
- Comprehension Cards
- Test Prep
- Test Tutor on *The Learning Site!* **www.harcourtschool.com**

Writing

- Direct instruction that emphasizes major **writing forms, purposes,** and **processes** and that connects reading to writing.
- Helpful suggestions to improve **organization** and **elaboration.**
- Systematic **grammar** and **spelling** instruction to develop proficiency in the conventions of writing.
- Frequent opportunities to **respond to literature** through writing.
- Opportunities for **research** and **inquiry** on self-selected and assigned topics.
- **Test preparation** to equip students for success on standardized and state tests.

Where to Find It

- Writing, Grammar, and Spelling lessons
- Building Literacy Skills
- Grammar and Spelling Practice Books
- Cross-Curricular Connections
- Test Prep

KNOW YOUR Students!

Formal and Informal Assessment

- ✔ *Reading Skills Assessment* including *Mid-Year* and *End-of-Year*
- ✔ *Placement and Individual Inventory Teacher's Guide*
- ✔ *Reading/Writing Performance Assessment*
- ✔ *Portfolio Assessment Teacher's Guide*
- ✔ *Holistic Reading Assessment*
- ✔ *Selection Comprehension Tests*
- ✔ Individual Reading Inventories in the *Teacher's Edition*
- ✔ Ongoing Informal Assessment
- ✔ Student Self- and Peer-Assessment

DINER

Reference Materials

Additional Resources

Videos and Technology

Introducing the Book

Invite students to discuss the title and the cover illustration. Ask what the title, *Journeys of Wonder*, might mean. Discuss where the dog in the picture might be going and what feeling the picture gives students.

You may want to share the following information about the cover artist, Mark Buehner:

Mark Buehner was born in Salt Lake City, Utah, and still lives there with his wife, author Caralyn Buehner, and their children. He has illustrated many award-winning children's books, including *Harvey Potter's Balloon Farm* and *Fanny's Dream*. Mark Buehner's art, which is created using oil paints and acrylics, has won him numerous awards, such as the Oradell Illustrators Award and the Society of Illustrators Silver Medal. For aspiring artists, Buehner's advice is, "Practice, practice, practice. Have fun with your art and do a lot of drawing all the time."

Predicting What's Inside

Discuss the letter to the reader Have students read the letter on page 1 of the *Student Edition*. Invite volunteers to give examples of interesting journeys that they have taken. Discuss how reading takes people on journeys of imagination.

Examine the organization of the book Ask students to preview the table of contents on pages 2–7. Have them point out the three theme titles and look at the selection titles and the book covers. Then ask them to make predictions about the kinds of selections they will be reading.

Examine the information at the end of the book Have students find the Glossary and the Index of Titles and Authors, beginning on page 362. Ask them how they can use these parts of the book. Pages R74 and R78 contain information about introducing students to the Glossary and the Index.

JOURNEYS OF WONDER

SENIOR AUTHORS
Roger C. Farr • Dorothy S. Strickland • Isabel L. Beck

AUTHORS
Richard F. Abrahamson • Alma Flor Ada • Bernice E. Cullinan • Margaret McKeown • Nancy Roser
Patricia Smith • Judy Wallis • Junko Yokota • Hallie Kay Yopp

SENIOR CONSULTANT
Asa G. Hilliard III

CONSULTANTS
Karen S. Kutiper • David A. Monti • Angelina Olivares

Harcourt
Orlando Boston Dallas Chicago San Diego

Visit *The Learning Site!*

www.harcourtschool.com

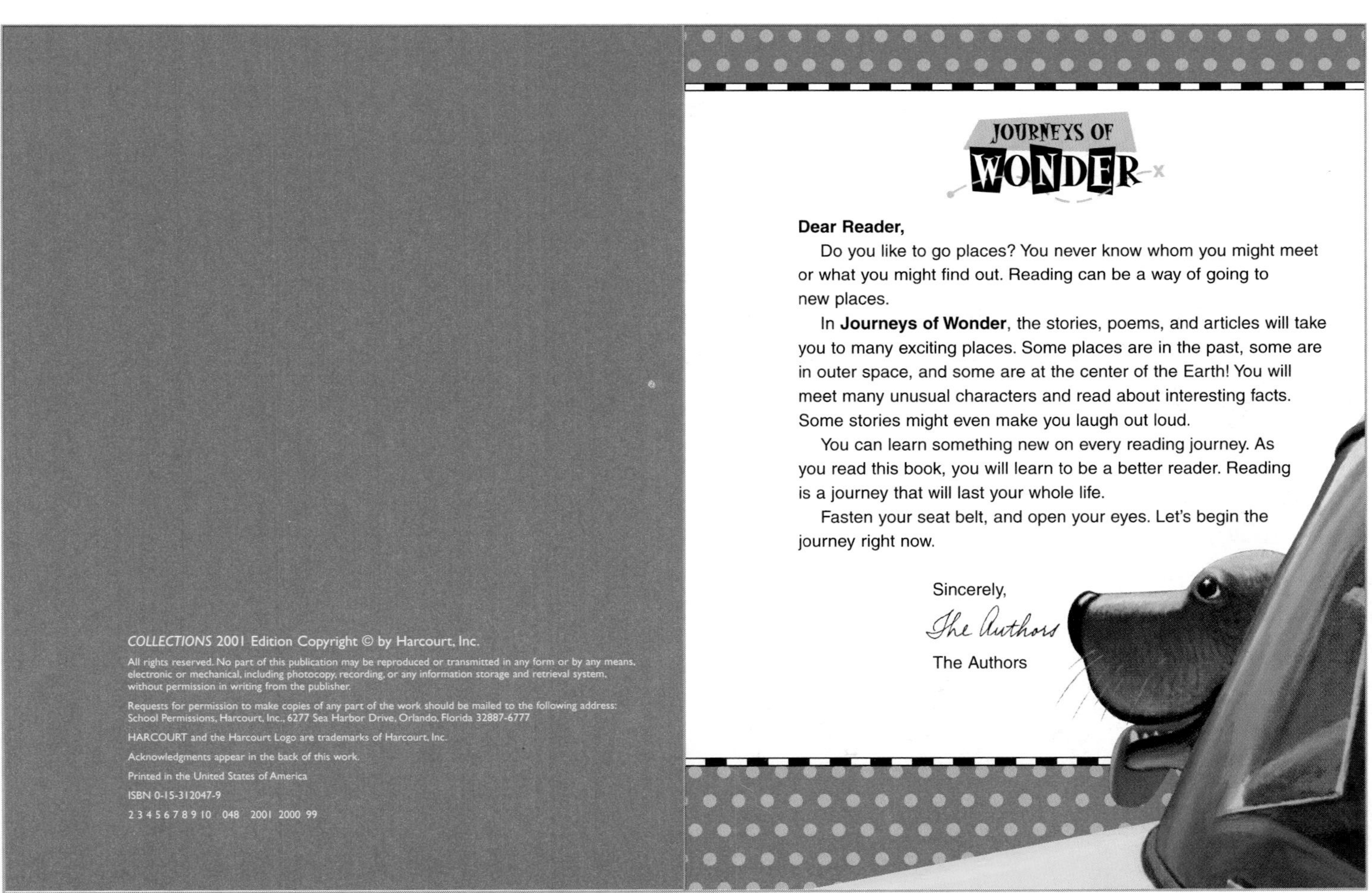

Acknowledgments appear in the back of this work.

Printed in the United States of America

ISBN 0-15-312047-9

2 3 4 5 6 7 8 9 10 048 2001 2000 99

JOURNEYS OF WONDER

Dear Reader,

Do you like to go places? You never know whom you might meet or what you might find out. Reading can be a way of going to new places.

In **Journeys of Wonder**, the stories, poems, and articles will take you to many exciting places. Some places are in the past, some are in outer space, and some are at the center of the Earth! You will meet many unusual characters and read about interesting facts. Some stories might even make you laugh out loud.

You can learn something new on every reading journey. As you read this book, you will learn to be a better reader. Reading is a journey that will last your whole life.

Fasten your seat belt, and open your eyes. Let's begin the journey right now.

Sincerely,

The Authors

The Authors

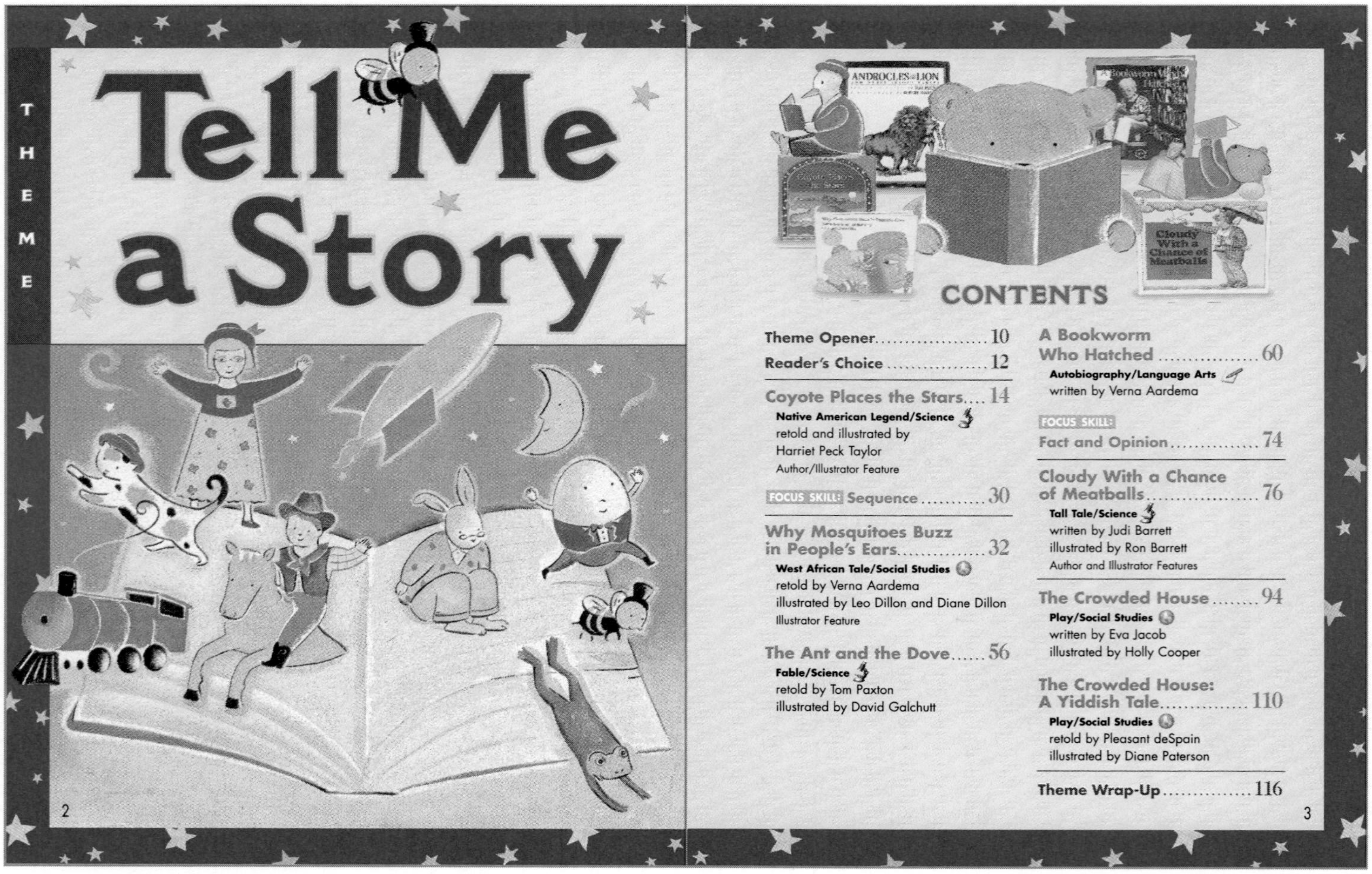

T H E M E

Tell Me a Story

2

CONTENTS

3

CONTENTS

5

THEME

Celebrate Our World

Contents

6

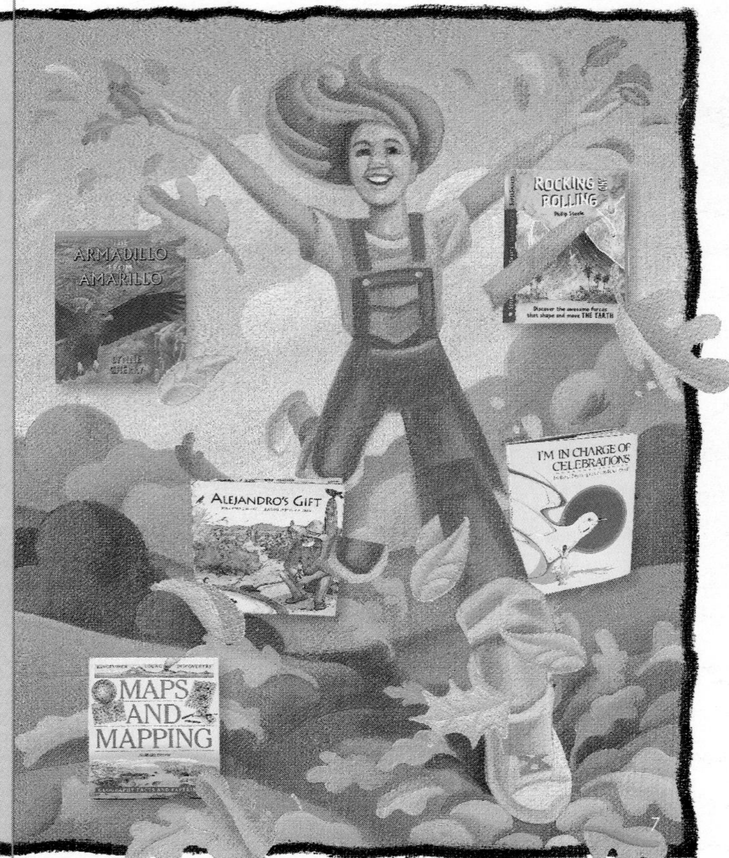

7

Using Reading Strategies

Introduce the Concept

Discuss with students what they do when they read. They may mention things that they do before, during, or after reading. Ask questions such as these: **What do you do to get yourself ready to read? What do you do when you don't understand something you are reading? What do you do when you come to a word you don't know?** Make a list on the board of students' answers. Tell students that they have named some good reading *strategies.* Explain that a strategy is a plan for doing something well.

EXPLAIN STRATEGIES GOOD READERS USE Have students read pages 8–9. Explain that these are the strategies they will be focusing on as they read the selections in this book. Discuss with students a brief explanation of each strategy:

- **Use Prior Knowledge** Think about what you already know about the topic and the kind of selection you are reading. For example, if you are reading an information book about tornadoes, think of what you already know about tornadoes. Think of what you know about information books, too. Using prior knowledge can help you set a purpose for reading—for example, to learn more about tornadoes.
- **Make and Confirm Predictions** Think about what might happen next in a story. Read to find out whether you are right. Make new predictions as you read.
- **Adjust Reading Rate** Think about the type of selection you are reading. A selection that has a lot of facts and details, such as a selection about volcanoes, may have to be read more slowly than a story about a character your age.
- **Self-Question** Have you ever found that you have questions as you are reading? Learn to ask yourself good questions as you read. This will help you check your understanding and focus on important ideas in the selection.
- **Create Mental Images** Sometimes, picturing in your mind what you are reading can help you understand and enjoy a selection. Pay attention to descriptive details.
- **Use Context to Confirm Meaning** After you read an unfamiliar or difficult word, ask yourself whether what you read makes sense in the sentence and whether it fits what is happening in the selection. By paying attention to the words around unfamiliar words, you can learn many new words and become a stronger reader.
- **Use Text Structure and Format** Find clues to meaning by looking at how the author organized the information. Look at headings and captions.
- **Use Graphic Aids** Sometimes a selection has graphic aids, such as pictures, graphs, charts, diagrams, maps, or time lines. These often show important information that can help you understand the selection.
- **Use Reference Sources** Use other books such as dictionaries and encyclopedias to help you understand unfamiliar words and ideas. You can also use them to check or confirm what you think something means.
- **Read Ahead** If you are having trouble understanding something in a selection, such as who a certain character is, don't give up. Keep on reading. The meaning may become clearer when you have more information.
- **Reread** If something doesn't make sense, you may have missed an important point. Try reading the passage again or going back to an earlier part of the selection.
- **Summarize** Tell or list the main points of the selection or the main things that happened. This will help you understand and remember what you read.

Using Reading Strategies

A strategy is a plan for doing something well.

You probably already use some strategies as you read. For example, you may **look at the title and pictures before you begin reading** a story. You may **think about what you want to find out while reading.** Using strategies like these can help you become a better reader.

Look at the list of strategies on page 9. You will learn about and use these strategies as you read the selections in this book. As you read, look back at the list to remind yourself of the **strategies good readers use.**

8

Strategies Good Readers Use

- Use Prior Knowledge
- Make and Confirm Predictions
- Adjust Reading Rate
- Self-Question
- Create Mental Images
- Use Context to Confirm Meaning
- Use Text Structure and Format
- Use Graphic Aids
- Use Reference Sources
- Read Ahead
- Reread
- Summarize

Here are some ways to check your own comprehension:

✔ Make a copy of this list on a piece of construction paper shaped like a bookmark.

✔ Have it handy as you read.

✔ After reading, talk with a classmate about which strategies you used and why.

9

Using Reading Strategies

MONITOR COMPREHENSION Distribute copies of Thinking About My Reading and My Reading Log, pages R97–R98. Have each student begin a personal reading portfolio. Students can use the forms to record how they choose self-selected books, the strategies they use during reading, and other reading behaviors.

STRATEGY BOOKMARK Have students make a bookmark from a sheet of heavy paper and write the strategies on the bookmark. Invite students to decorate their bookmarks. As they read, they should refer to the bookmark to help remind them of the strategies they can use.

READING NOTEBOOK Explain to students that they should keep a reading notebook to record their responses to selections and to monitor their progress as readers. They may use a spiral-bound notebook or sheets of paper stapled together. In the notebook, they should create sections to write about which strategies work best for them and to develop their own plans for reading different kinds of selections. You may want to have them record how long they read each day. They should also set aside a section of the notebook for a vocabulary log, where they will list new or interesting words they come across in their reading.

THEME 1

Tell Me a Story

In this theme, students learn that storytelling takes many forms and serves many purposes. As they read stories and meet storytellers from around the world, they discover new ways to tell their own stories.

Theme Resources

The following resources can help you provide regular, frequent opportunities for every student to read and listen to literature.

INSTRUCTIONAL-LEVEL READING

STUDENT EDITION: JOURNEYS OF WONDER

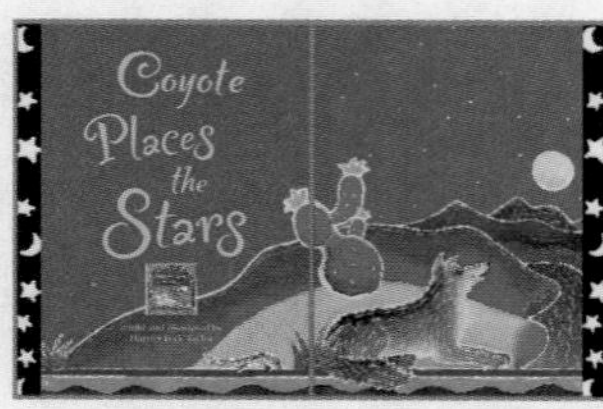

"Coyote Places the Stars," pages 14–27

"Why Mosquitoes Buzz in People's Ears," pages 32–55

"The Ant and the Dove," pages 56–57

"A Bookworm Who Hatched," pages 60–71

"Cloudy With a Chance of Meatballs," pages 76–91

"The Crowded House," pages 94–109

"The Crowded House: A Yiddish Tale," pages 110–113

All selections are available on *Literature Cassettes 3 and 4*.

EASY READER: NEW ADVENTURES

"Many Moons Ago," pages 126–133

"Grandpa Tells Why," pages 134–141

"This Is My Story, " pages 142–149

"The Big Snow," pages 150–157

"Good Advice," pages 158–165

INDEPENDENT/SELF-SELECTED READING

READER'S CHOICE LIBRARY

The Wave by Margaret Hodges

What Do Authors Do? by Eileen Christelow

TAKE-HOME BOOKS

Phaeton and the Chariot of the Sun

The World Next Door

You Won't Believe What Happened Today!

What If the Rain Were Doughnuts?

Paul Bunyan Moves Out

See also Independent and Self-Selected Reading, page T11, and the Leveled Library.

LISTENING SELECTIONS

READ-ALOUD ANTHOLOGY

"How the Girl Taught the Coyotes to Sing Harmony" *by Nancy Wood*

"The Clever Warthog" retold *by George Schaller*

"Garrett A. Morgan" *by Wade Hudson*

"Big Moon Tortilla" *by Joy Cowley*

"Rudolph Is Tired of the City" *by Gwendolyn Brooks*

READ ALOUD TO STUDENTS

LISTENING TO LITERATURE

"The Storyteller" collected by Harold Courlander and Wolf Leslau, pages T6–T9

TECHNOLOGY CONNECTIONS

***Phonics Express*™ CD-ROM**
Vowel variants: /o͞o/*oo*, /o͝o/*oo*, *ou*; vowel variant: /o͞o/*ou*, *ough*; soft c: final /s/*ce*, initial /s/*ce*, *ci*, *cy*; soft g: final /j/*ge*, *dge*, initial /j/*ge*, *gi*, *gy*; structural analysis (suffixes *-ly*, *-ful*, *-ness*)

Videocassettes
Astronomy 101 ©1994. Library Video Company, 25 min. *Patricia Polacco Dream Keeper* (Searchlight Films) ©1996. Library Video Company, 23 min.

Student activities:
Building Background, Bonus Words, Author Information, Skill Activities, Test Tutor, Computer Station

Teacher resources:
Link Bank, Graphic Organizers, Multi-Level Resources

Reaching All Learners

Customizing Instruction

Make use of these flexible grouping strategies to keep all students on task while you provide direct instruction to a few:

During...	Some students can...
Introducing Vocabulary	• Create a word web of theme-related words. • Look up the Bonus Words activity on *The Learning Site* at **www.harcourtschool.com**
Preteaching the Skill	• Read aloud a selection with a partner and use a Comprehension Card together. • Complete a Listening to Literature activity.
Writing/Grammar/Spelling	• Read a Leveled Library book. • Revise the *Daily Language Practice* sentences. • Complete a page in their *Grammar Practice Books.*

INQUIRY PROJECT

Throughout this theme, you will see several opportunities for **Inquiry Projects.** Suggestions can be found on pages T51, T103, T143, T187, and T233.

Theme Project

CLASS STORIES Remind students that stories are told around the world. Often, a simple plot will appear in the stories of many cultures. Give groups of students the story lines below, and have each group member write his or her own story. Encourage students to include elements of their cultures in their stories. Have them compare the stories when everyone has finished. Ask them what story elements are the same and why some elements are different.

- Story 1: Someone is locked in a tower.
- Story 2: A king or queen tries to destroy a rival.
- Story 3: A poor but clever person saves the kingdom from a monster.

Have students bind their stories together, add a cover and a title, and display their book in the classroom library.

MATERIALS

- pencils
- markers
- notebook paper
- computer paper, printer, and word-processing program (if available)
- 3-ring binder
- 3-hole punch
- colored paper for cover

from Journaling in the Intermediate Grades

by Dr. Donna M. Ogle

Daily journals help students learn to write about their own experiences and thoughts. Many teachers have students keep spiral notebooks in their desks and use the first few moments of the day or of the class to put their own thinking on paper. In addition, if some class members get upset or get involved in an argument, the teacher can turn to the journals and let each child write out his or her feelings.

Teachers can also have students use daily journals as the starting point for more structured writing. Ideas that students are thinking about can be saved for elaboration later. Suggestions for writing prompts can be developed by the class. Here are some examples:

- Reflect on what you are learning and how you are learning it.
- Explain what things you are most interested in currently and keep a record so you can know yourself better.
- What are your goals for today?

Reading Is Fun

Reading *is* fun, but sometimes readers feel the opposite as they struggle to improve their reading. The question is how to encourage young readers to feel safe with books on their reading level. Here are some ways to help them feel safe to try a book:

- *Buddy reading.* Ask your third graders to read aloud to younger, beginning readers. This system works well in multi-age classrooms. Both students benefit: the older one (who chooses the book on his or her reading level) has the chance to practice reading aloud, and the younger one has the opportunity to listen.
- *Classroom library materials.* Vary the reading materials—books, newspapers, magazines—in your classroom so that readers feel safe choosing anything of interest to read. Have a choice of topics, genres, reading levels, and formats in materials that teacher and peers will approve of.
- *SSR.* Even Ramona's teacher in *Ramona Quimby, Age 8* promoted Sustained Silent Reading. She called it "D.E.A.R." or "Drop Everything and Read." Everyone feels safe to enjoy any book during this time of the school day. And all of your readers will know that joy of reading.

The grade-level themes in ***Collections*** are based on universal themes that align across all grades in the same order. This order facilitates theme-based learning in multi-age environments and combination classrooms. The universal theme for Tell Me a Story is *Creativity*.

READ ALOUD TO STUDENTS

The Storyteller

by Harold Courlander

GENRE: **FOLKTALE**

Selection Summary: The king of Shoa has heard just about every story ever told. Desperate to hear something new, he says that he will reward the storyteller who can make him cry "Enough! No more!" with land and a title. Many men try but fail. One day, a simple farmer begins a tale of a peasant storing wheat in a granary. Ants find a hole in the granary, and one by one, carry away grains of wheat to their anthill. As the farmer gives details about each ant, the king grows more and more upset, until he cries "Enough!" and the farmer wins.

AUTHOR PROFILE

Harold Courlander is a novelist and one of this country's foremost scholars of the oral tradition. He has written about and collected legends, folktales, and music of West Africa, East Africa, Asia, the Pacific Islands, the Middle East, Haiti, and the Hopi Indians.

1 What is the king's problem?

Once there was a king in the land of Shoa who loved nothing so much as listening to stories. Every moment of his spare time was spent in listening to the tales told by the storytellers of the country, but a time came when there were no stories left that he hadn't heard. His hunger for stories came to be known in the neighboring kingdoms, and wandering singers and storytellers came to Shoa to be rewarded for whatever new tales they could bring. But the more tales the king heard the fewer were left that he had not heard. And so, finally, in desperation he let it be known throughout the land that whatever storyteller could make him cry, "Enough! No more!" would receive a great piece of land and the title of Ras, or prince.

Many men, inspired by the thought of such wealth and honors, came to tell him stories, but always he sat and listened eagerly without ever protesting that he had had too much.

But one day a farmer came and offered to tell stories until the king was so full of them that he would cry out in protest. The king smiled.

2 What does the king think of the farmer's chances?

"The best storytellers in Ethiopia have come and gone without telling me enough," he said. "And now you come in your simple innocence to win the land and the title of Ras. Well, begin, you may try."

And so the farmer settled himself comfortably on a rug and began:

"Once there was a peasant who sowed wheat," he said. "He mowed it when it was grown, threshed it, and put all the precious grain in his granary. It was a rich harvest, one of the best he had ever had.

"But, and this is the irony of the tale, in his granary there was a tiny flaw, a hole big enough to pass a straw through. And when the grain was all stored an ant came and went through the hole and found the wheat. He carried away a single grain of it to his anthill to eat."

"Ah-ha!" the king said, showing interest. For this story was one that he hadn't heard.

"The next day," the farmer continued, "another ant came through the hole and found the wheat, and he, too, carried away a grain of it."

"Ah-ha!" the king said.

"The next day another ant came and carried away a grain," the farmer said.

"Ah-ha!"

"The next day still another ant came and carried away a grain."

"Yes, yes, I understand, let us get on with the story," the king said.

"The next day another ant came, and carried away another grain. And the next day another ant came and carried away another grain."

3 When the king says, "The story is the thing," what does he mean?

"Let us not dally with the details," the king said. "The story is the thing."

"The next day another ant came," the farmer continued.

"Please," the king said, "please!"

"But there are so many ants in the story," the farmer said. "And the next day another ant came for a grain of wheat, and . . ."

"No, no, it must not be!" the king said.

"Ah, but it is the crux of the story," the farmer replied. "And the next day another ant came and took away a grain . . ."

"But I understand all this," the king protested. "Let us pass over it and get on with the plot."

ACCESS PRIOR KNOWLEDGE

Use these suggestions to help students make connections between the selection and what they know:

- Remind students that folktales are often passed on from generation to generation within a culture before being written down. Many folktales teach a life-lesson to the listener. Have students name stories they have heard or read that teach a lesson. (Students may mention Aesop's fables or other similar tales.)
- "The Storyteller" is an example of a traditional tale common to many cultures. It involves a challenge put before the people by their ruler. Ask students for names of other such tales.
- Display a map of the world. Have a volunteer locate Ethiopia on the map. Discuss with students the location and climate of the country, and have them keep this in mind as they listen to the story.

SET A PURPOSE FOR LISTENING

Remind students that this story is a folktale. Point out that some folktales are universal—they deal with themes and situations that could take place anywhere. As students listen, ask them to think of changes that would be needed to set this tale in Europe, Asia, or North America. Have them also decide on their main purpose for listening. (Possible response: to enjoy and appreciate.)

STRATEGY REMINDER

Concentrate on the Speaker Ask students to pay close attention to your tone of voice as you read. Your tone will serve to explain what the characters in this story are feeling.

LISTENING STRATEGIES

- **Concentrate on the Speaker**
- Separate Fact from Opinion
- Keep an Open Mind
- Self-Question
- Create Mental Images

Listen Responsively Use the questions in the margins to assess students' understanding and appreciation of the selection. You can also look for nonverbal cues such as head-nodding to make sure students are concentrating on the story.

Develop Vocabulary Through Listening Have students listen for these unfamiliar farming words: *sowed, threshed, granary*. Ask them to try to decipher those words' meanings from the context of the sentence or paragraph.

Tip for Reading Aloud Help students recognize characters' feelings by using your voice to emphasize the king's increasing annoyance with the farmer's long, drawn-out tale.

"And the next day another ant came and took his grain. And the next day . . ."

4 In the farmer's story, what would happen the next day?

"Stop, I want no more of it!" the king shouted.

"The story must be told in the proper way," the farmer said. "Besides, the granary is still nearly full of wheat, and it must be emptied. That is in the story. And the next day . . ."

"No, no, enough, enough!" the king shouted.

"And the next day another ant . . ."

"Enough, enough, you may have the land and the title of Ras!" the king shouted, jumping up and fleeing from the room.

So the farmer became a prince and owned a great parcel of land.

This is what people mean when they say: "One grain at a time brings good fortune."

Responding to the Literature

RETELL THE FOLKTALE THROUGH DANCE

Have students work in groups of four to make up a dance that tells the story. Two students can be the rhythm section, and two can dance the parts of the king and the farmer. Remind them that repetition is the key to the farmer's story, and repetition should therefore be part of their dance.

WRITE A FUNNY STORY

Have students work in pairs to write funny stories. Explain that the story should be so silly that it makes readers laugh. Student partners should start by brainstorming a funny situation. Then they should use an outline like this one to organize their ideas:

1. Who, Where, and When
2. What Happened
3. How It Turned Out

EXTEND VOCABULARY

Ask students to retell the farmer's story in their own words. Tell them to use in their retelling the vocabulary words *sowed*, *threshed*, and *granary*, which they found for Develop Vocabulary Through Listening. If necessary, reread the farmer's story first, and have students use a dictionary to locate the meaning of each word.

DISCUSS THE SELECTION

1. **Do you think the farmer wins fairly? Explain your answer.** (Possible responses: Yes, he succeeds in making the king cry "Enough!"; no, he tricks the king by telling a story with no end.) CRITICAL: EXPRESS PERSONAL OPINIONS/MAKE JUDGMENTS
2. **Why does this story fit the theme?** (Possible response: The theme is Tell Me a Story, and that is what the king asks; the farmer is the storyteller.) CRITICAL: INTERPRET THEME/RETURN TO PURPOSE
3. **Have you ever heard or read a tale that was similar to this? Explain how it was similar and different.** (Responses will vary. Encourage students to think of tales with kings as characters, set long ago, and involving a prize.)

RETELL/SUMMARIZE

Discuss with students sections of the selection that seem unclear. Use a sequence chart to put the events in order. Then ask students to summarize the story by acting out the order of important events. Have them write one-sentence summaries of the selection and compare and contrast their sentences.

THEME

Tell Me a Story

CONTENTS

10 11

Preview the Theme

DISCUSS THE THEME CONTENTS Have students examine the table of contents for the theme and talk about familiar authors or titles listed there. Have students identify the title of one selection they are most interested in reading and tell why that title appeals to them. Ask volunteers to read the theme title and predict what the selections will have in common.

QUICKWRITE

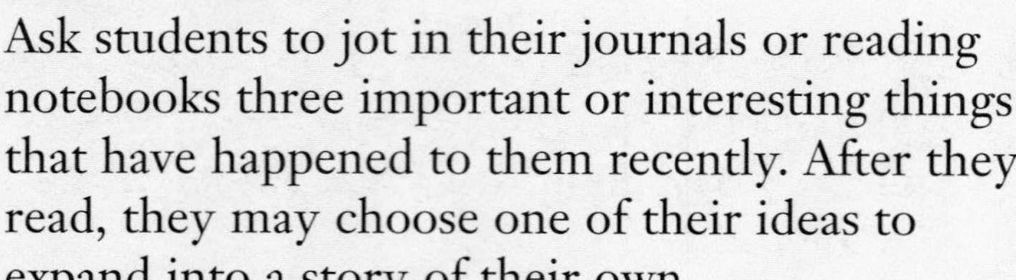

Ask students to jot in their journals or reading notebooks three important or interesting things that have happened to them recently. After they read, they may choose one of their ideas to expand into a story of their own.

BEGIN AN ONGOING GRAPHIC ORGANIZER Invite students to begin creating a graphic organizer that will help them keep track of some reasons for storytelling. You may want to keep the organizer on a computer, a chart, or a bulletin board. Tell them to return to it periodically as they read the selections in the theme to add new ideas or information.

What stories have I told or heard recently, and what was the purpose of each?

TO EXPLAIN	TO ENTERTAIN	TO PERSUADE
• a story about why the sky is blue	• a story about a mouse on skis	• a story about a person who learns a lesson

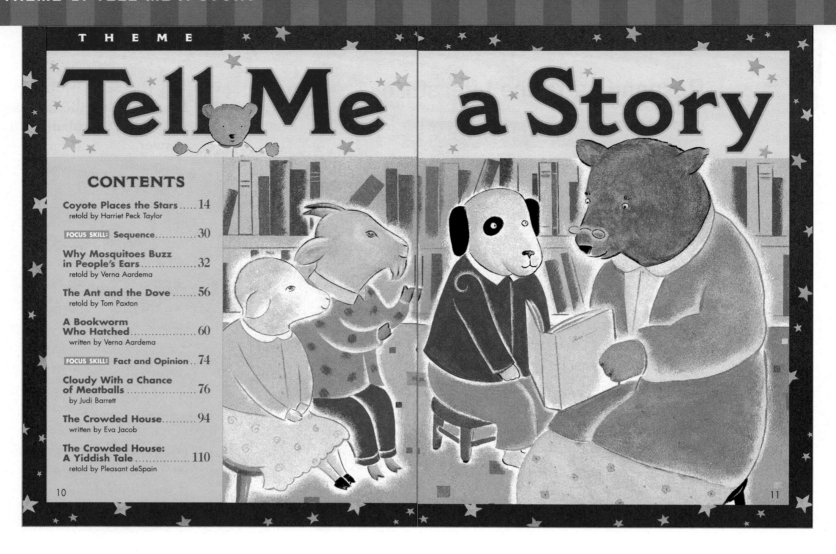

Reader's Choice

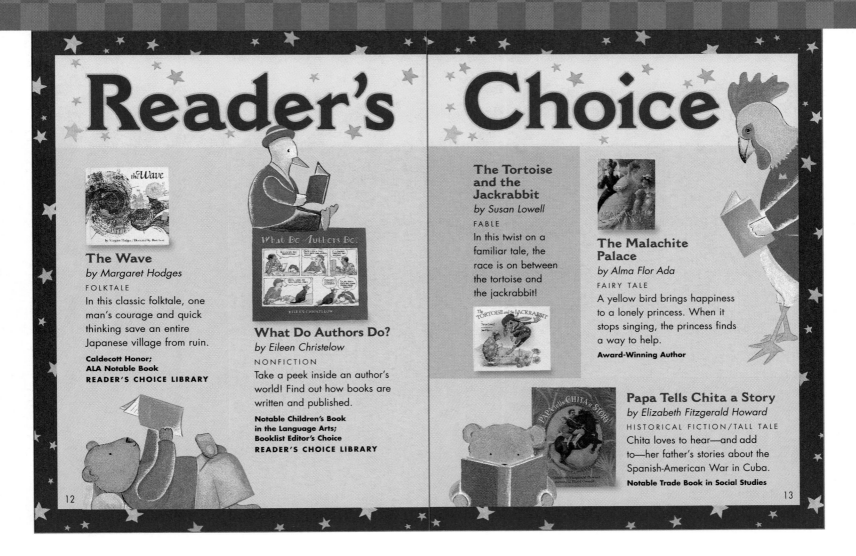

The Wave
by Margaret Hodges
FOLKTALE
In this classic folktale, one man's courage and quick thinking save an entire Japanese village from ruin.
Caldecott Honor;
ALA Notable Book
READER'S CHOICE LIBRARY

What Do Authors Do?
by Eileen Christelow
NONFICTION
Take a peek inside an author's world! Find out how books are written and published.
Notable Children's Book in the Language Arts;
Booklist Editor's Choice
READER'S CHOICE LIBRARY

12

The Tortoise and the Jackrabbit
by Susan Lowell
FABLE
In this twist on a familiar tale, the race is on between the tortoise and the jackrabbit!

The Malachite Palace
by Alma Flor Ada
FAIRY TALE
A yellow bird brings happiness to a lonely princess. When it stops singing, the princess finds a way to help.
Award-Winning Author

Papa Tells Chita a Story
by Elizabeth Fitzgerald Howard
HISTORICAL FICTION/TALL TALE
Chita loves to hear—and add to—her father's stories about the Spanish-American War in Cuba.
Notable Trade Book in Social Studies

13

Independent and Self-Selected Reading

The Tortoise and the Jackrabbit by Susan Lowell EASY

Papa Tells Chita a Story by Elizabeth Fitzgerald Howard AVERAGE

The Wave by Margaret Hodges AVERAGE

What Do Authors Do? by Eileen Christelow AVERAGE

The Malachite Palace by Alma Flor Ada CHALLENGING

PREVIEW READER'S CHOICE BOOKS Have students read the book titles aloud, and ask volunteers to provide information or opinions about familiar authors or books. Point out the genre labels and ask volunteers to give examples of other books or selections that share that genre. (Responses will vary.) CRITICAL: CLASSIFY

CHOOSE TRADE BOOKS Have students use the following questions to help them select books to read:

- Do I prefer fiction or nonfiction?
- Does the first page of the book draw me in?
- Could I learn something new by reading this book?
- Have I read and enjoyed a book like this one before?

MONITOR COMPREHENSION Distribute Thinking About My Reading, page R97, and have students complete it to monitor their own comprehension and their use of reading strategies.

TRADE BOOK LESSON PLANS See the Reader's Choice Library lesson plans on pages T236–T239. For more detailed lessons, see the *Leveled Library Teacher's Guide.*

LESSON PREVIEW

"Coyote Places the Stars"

THEME
Tell Me a Story

GENRE
Pourquoi Tale

- A kind of **folktale**
- **Explains why** something in the natural world came to be the way it is
- Usually has **animal characters**

CROSS-CURRICULAR CONNECTIONS

- **SCIENCE:** Searching for the Great Bear
- **ART:** The Batik Technique

FOCUS STRATEGY SELF-QUESTION

- **Before Reading:** Strategy Reminder on page T21
- **During Reading:** Apply the Strategy on pages T26, T32

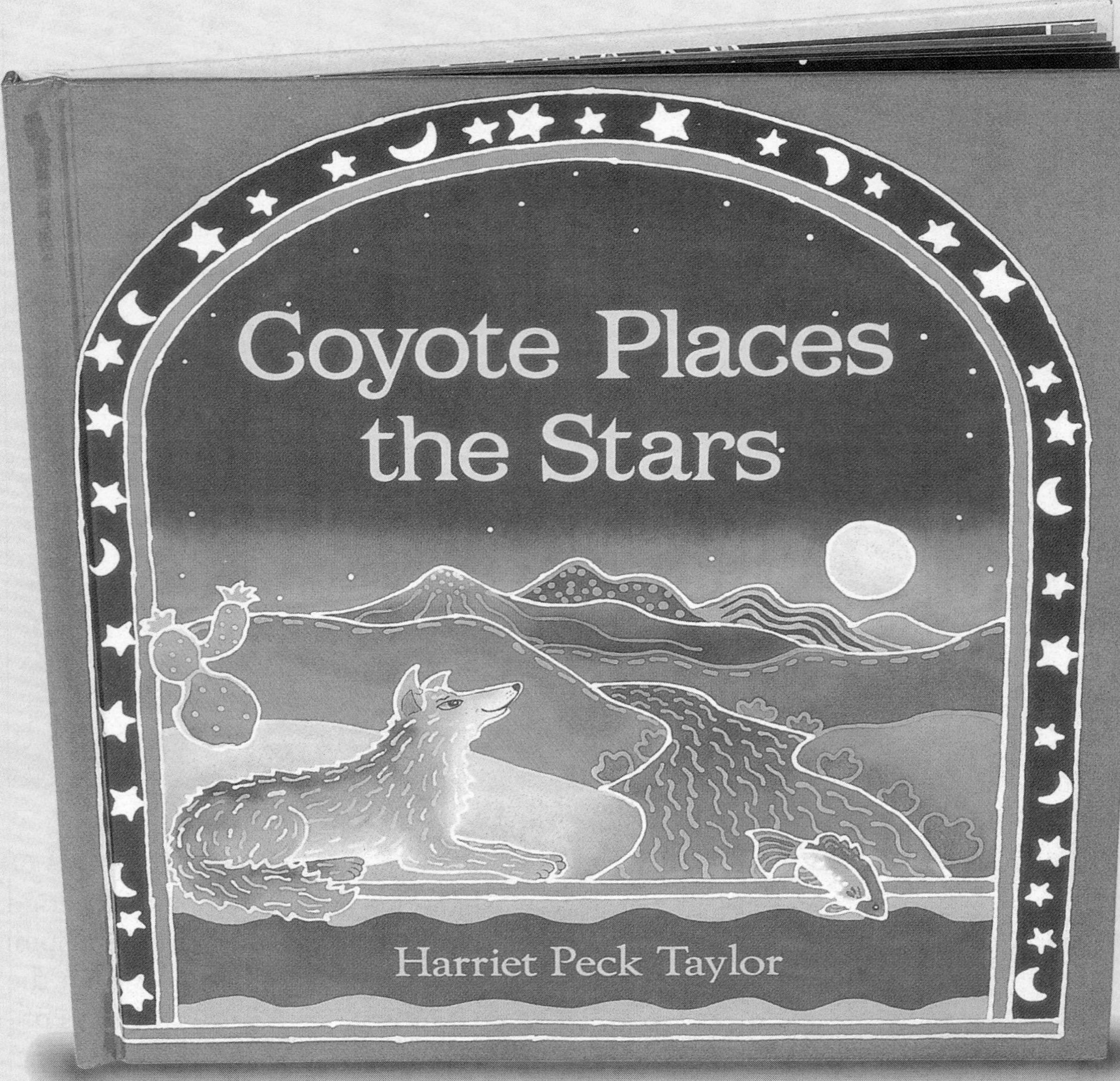

FOCUS SKILL SEQUENCE

- **Before Reading:** Introduce the Skill on pages T20–T21
- **During Reading:** Apply the Skill on pages T26, T32
- **After Reading:** Practice the Skill on pages T40–T41 (*Student Edition* 30–31)

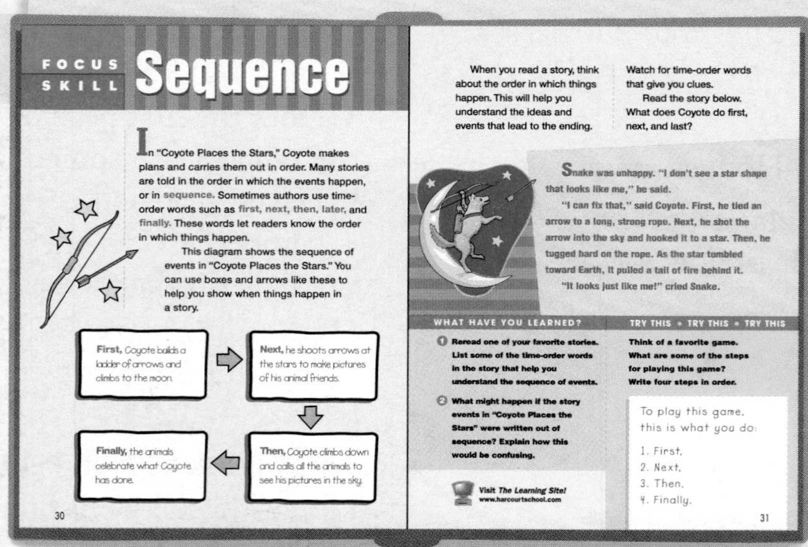

FOCUS SKILL **Sequence**

In "Coyote Places the Stars," Coyote makes plans and carries them out in order. Many stories are told in the order in which the events happen, or in **sequence**. Sometimes authors use time-order words such as **first, next, then, later,** and **finally.** These words let readers know the order in which things happen.

This diagram shows the sequence of events in "Coyote Places the Stars." You can use boxes and arrows like these to help you show when things happen in a story.

First, Coyote builds a ladder of arrows and climbs to the moon. → **Next,** he shoots arrows at the stars to make pictures of his animal friends. → **Then,** Coyote climbs down and calls all the animals to see his pictures in the sky. → **Finally,** the animals celebrate what Coyote has done.

30

When you read a story, think about the order in which things happen. This will help you understand the ideas and events that lead to the ending. Watch for time-order words that give you clues.

Read the story below. What does Coyote do first, next, and last?

Snake was unhappy. "I don't see a star shape that looks like me," he said.

"I can fix that," said Coyote. First, he tied an arrow to a long, strong rope. Next, he shot the arrow into the sky and hooked it to a star. Then, he tugged hard on the rope. As the star tumbled toward Earth, it pulled a tail of fire behind it.

"It looks just like me!" cried Snake.

WHAT HAVE YOU LEARNED?

1. **Reread one of your favorite stories. List some of the time-order words in the story that help you understand the sequence of events.**
2. **What might happen if the story events in "Coyote Places the Stars" were written out of sequence? Explain how this would be confusing.**

Visit *The Learning Site!* www.harcourtschool.com

TRY THIS • TRY THIS • TRY THIS

Think of a favorite game. What are some of the steps for playing this game? Write four steps in order.

To play this game, this is what you do:

1. First,
2. Next,
3. Then,
4. Finally,

31

▲ **Student Edition, pages 30–31**

As students read "Coyote Places the Stars," they will learn that some folktales were told long ago to explain the natural world.

Selection Summary

In this selection, based on a traditional Native American pourquoi tale, Coyote creates and then climbs a ladder of arrows to the moon. Discovering that he can place the stars where he likes by shooting arrows, he arranges constellations in the images of himself and his friends. He summons the other animals with his howls and they honor him with a feast. Today, the coyote's howls still call us to look at the stars.

Author/Illustrator Profile

Harriet Peck Taylor has been a professional artist since she graduated with Fine Arts and Arts in Education degrees from the University of Colorado. In 1982, she began working as a textile designer and gradually developed her present style, which she describes as "naïve and primitive." Her illustrations appear in her nationally recognized children's books.

BELOW-LEVEL READERS

EASY READER
"Many Moons Ago," pp. 126–133. Reinforces selection vocabulary and these additional words from "Coyote Places the Stars":

clever arrows pictures moon star

See *New Adventures Intervention Reader Teacher's Guide,* pages 92–97.

CASSETTE
"Coyote Places the Stars" is available on *Literature Cassette 3.*

CHALLENGE

READER'S CHOICE LIBRARY
Earth: Our Planet in Space by Seymour Simon. CHALLENGING

INQUIRY PROJECTS
See page T51. Encourage students to pose questions they would like to have answered. They can then plan and carry out research to answer their questions.

SUGGESTED
LESSON PLANNER

COYOTE PLACES THE STARS

Skills and Strategies

Reading
Listening
Speaking
Viewing

Vocabulary
- canyon
- pride
- swiftly
- skillful
- feast
- gazing
- arranged

PRETEACHING AND READING — DAY 1

BUILDING BACKGROUND AND CONCEPTS T18

INTRODUCING VOCABULARY T19
Transparency 1
Practice Book p. 3
■ Vocabulary Station

PRETEACHING SKILLS
Before Reading
✔ FOCUS SKILL Sequence (Introduce) T20–T21
Transparency 2
FOCUS STRATEGY Self-Question T21

PREREADING STRATEGIES T22

READING THE SELECTION T22–T35
Literature Cassette 3
Author Information T35

ALTERNATIVE SELECTION

Easy Reader: "Many Moons Ago"

NOTE: Students may begin reading the selection on Day 2.

READING AND RESPONDING — DAY 2

LITERARY RESPONSE T34
Return to the Predictions/Purpose
Appreciating the Literature

THINK ABOUT IT T34

RETELL AND SUMMARIZE T35
Practice Book p. 5

GRAMMAR
Object Pronouns (Review) T25

REREADING FOR FLUENCY
Record a Story T38
■ Recording Station

LITERATURE RESPONSE
Sequence of Instructions T38

INTERVENTION STRATEGIES FOR BELOW-LEVEL READERS T39
FOCUS STRATEGY Rereading
Language Exploration

	Day 1	Day 2
Writing	**Informative Writing: Paragraph That Compares** Connect Writing to Reading T44	Teach/Model T44 Analyze the Model *Transparency 3* *Language Handbook* pp. 48–49, 53
Grammar	**Adjectives** Teach/Model T46 *Transparency 5* *Language Handbook* pp. 116–117	Extend the Concept T46 *Grammar Practice Book* p. 58
Daily Language Practice	**1. Some starrs in the sky look like a drawing of a bare.** (stars; bear) **2. how did these shaps come to be** (How; shapes; be?)	**1. Coyote moved the stars by shooting arrows at they.** (them) **2. Coyotes star fourms looked like animales.** (Coyote's; forms; animals)
Spelling	**Words with /ôr/** form, fourth, war, storm, horse, warn, morning, forest, court, porch Pretest/Self-Check T48 *Transparency 7*	Teach/Model T48 *Practice Book* p. 10 Handwriting Tip

KEY
✔ **Tested Skills**
■ **Management Option:** See Managing the Classroom, page T16, for ongoing independent activities.

Reaching All Learners: Support for "Many Moons Ago," an alternative selection, appears on *Intervention Reader Teacher's Guide*, pp. 92–97.

READING AND RESPONDING

DAY 3

RESPONSE ACTIVITIES
Write an Announcement T36
Draw a Constellation T37
Write a Song T37
Write a Letter T37

Selection Comprehension Test

VOCABULARY
Homographs and Homophones (Review) T27
Practice Book p. 4

ORAL LANGUAGE
Tell a Round-Robin Tale T38
Activity Card 31, R13

VIEWING
Reflected Light T38

INDEPENDENT READING
Reader's Choice Library: *Jordi's Star* T17

Reader's Choice Library Book ▶

Writing Prompts T44
Prewrite and Draft T45
Transparency 4
ClarisWorks for Kids®

Oral Review/Practice T47
Grammar Practice Book p. 59

1. **Us sat on the poarch and watched the rain.** (We; porch)
2. **during stoormes you cannot see the sky.** (During storms)

Spelling Strategies T49
Apply to Writing
Spelling Practice Book p. 46

EXTENDING SKILLS & STRATEGIES

DAY 4

COMPREHENSION
After Reading
✔ FOCUS SKILL Sequence (Introduce) T40–T41
Practice Book pp. 6–7

DECODING/PHONICS
Vowel Variants: /o͞o/, /o͝o/ (Review) T29

VOCABULARY T42–T43
Reviewing Vocabulary Words
Extending Vocabulary
Practice Book p. 8

TAKE-HOME BOOK
Phaeton and the Chariot of the Sun T42

CROSS-CURRICULAR CONNECTIONS
Science: Searching for the Great Bear T50
Activity Card 32, R13

Take-Home Book ▶

Revise T45

Apply to Writing T47
Practice Book p. 9

1. **how bright the full moon is?** (How; is!)
2. **i can see only foar large stars.** (I; four)

Spelling Activities T49
Spelling Practice Book p. 47

EXTENDING SKILLS & STRATEGIES

DAY 5

COMPREHENSION
✔ Story Elements (Maintain) T31

CROSS-CURRICULAR CONNECTIONS
Art: The Batik Technique T51
✔ FOCUS SKILL Apply Sequence

Inquiry Projects T51
COMPUTER STATION T16
Research
■ Research Station

SELF-SELECTED READING T17
- *Coyote Steals the Blanket*
- *Fire Race: A Karuk Coyote Tale*
- Leveled Library Book: *Coyote and the Laughing Butterflies*

Leveled Library Book ▲

Assessment T45
Student Self- and Peer-Assessment
Scoring Rubric

Cumulative Review T47
Grammar Practice Book p. 60

1. **you and me will sing a song.** (You and I)
2. **Do you sing in the choorus.** (chorus?)

Posttest T49

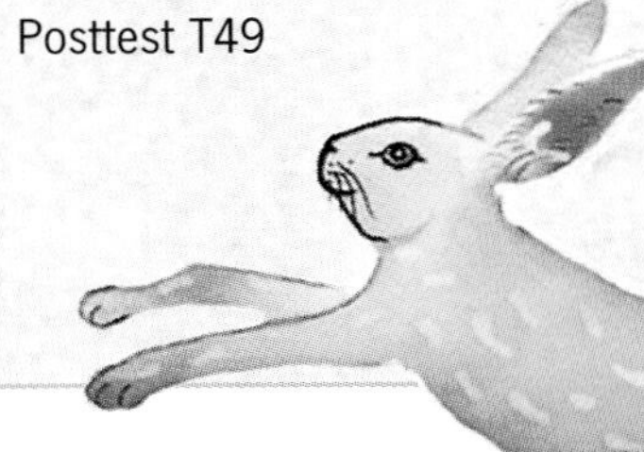

Visit *The Learning Site!*
www.harcourtschool.com

Managing the Classroom

While you provide direct instruction to individuals or small groups, other students can work on ongoing activities like the ones below.

Recording Station

OBJECTIVE
To develop and improve oral reading skills

MATERIALS
- tape recorder
- audiocassettes

See page T38 for the Rereading Activity. Groups of students can tape-record a complete rereading of "Coyote Places the Stars" to share with younger students. Have them practice their parts by rereading them several times until they can read fluently and automatically.

Vocabulary Station

OBJECTIVE
To collect verbs that describe animal behavior

MATERIALS
- index cards
- markers
- thesaurus

Have students make an illustrated index card for each animal in the story. They should list on the card verbs that tell how the animal moves and sounds. They should consult a thesaurus to find synonyms.

Research Station

OBJECTIVE
To use fiction and nonfiction books to find information

MATERIALS
- books about the constellations
- books about batik
- books about coyotes
- books of Native American tales

Students can use nonfiction books and books of folktales for the Inquiry Projects they choose. (See page T51.) Have them start a bibliography for each topic and add the titles of relevant books as they find them.

Computer Station

OBJECTIVE
To use the Internet to learn more about batik art

MATERIALS
- computer with Internet access and a printer

Before students complete the batik activity on page T51, they can use the Internet to view both professional and student batik artworks. Also suggest that they use a Web search engine to find and print a picture if they would like to start with a pattern.

Visit *The Learning Site!*
www.harcourtschool.com

Note: For more options, see pages T36–T37, T38–T39, and T50–T51.

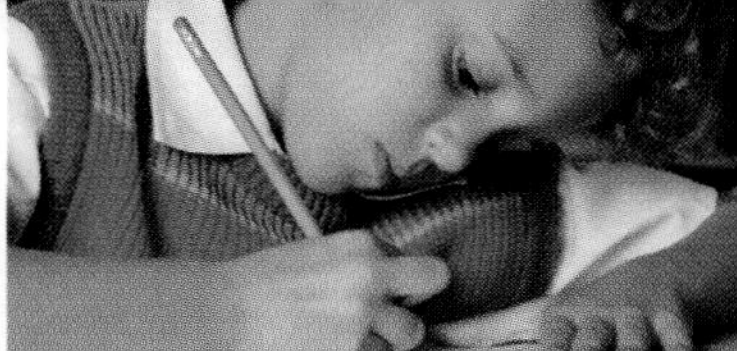

GUIDED READING

Multi-Level Books

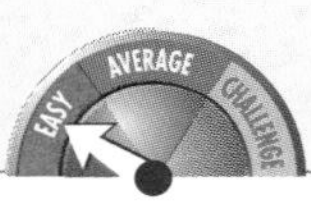

EASY

The Big Dipper by Franklyn M. Branley. HarperCollins, 1991. NONFICTION: CONSTELLATIONS

Coyote Steals the Blanket by Janet Stevens. Holiday House, 1993. FOLKTALE: COYOTE AS TRICKSTER

EASY READER: NEW ADVENTURES
"Many Moons Ago," pp. 126–133. FOLKTALE: MOON LORE

TAKE-HOME BOOK
Phaeton and the Chariot of the Sun FICTION: GREEK MYTH

AVERAGE

Fire Race: A Karuk Coyote Tale by Jonathan London. Chronicle, 1993. FOLKTALE: COYOTE AS TRICKSTER

Stargazers by Gail Gibbons. Holiday House, 1992. NONFICTION: STARS

LEVELED LIBRARY BOOK
Coyote and the Laughing Butterflies by Harriet Peck Taylor. FOLKTALE: SELECTION AUTHOR

READER'S CHOICE LIBRARY
Jordi's Star by Alma Flor Ada. FICTION: STARS

See the **Reader's Choice Library lesson plan** on pages T754–T755.

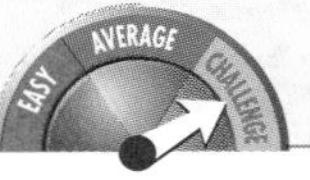

CHALLENGING

The Magic School Bus Lost in the Solar System by Joanna Cole. Scholastic, 1992. NONFICTION: SOLAR SYSTEM

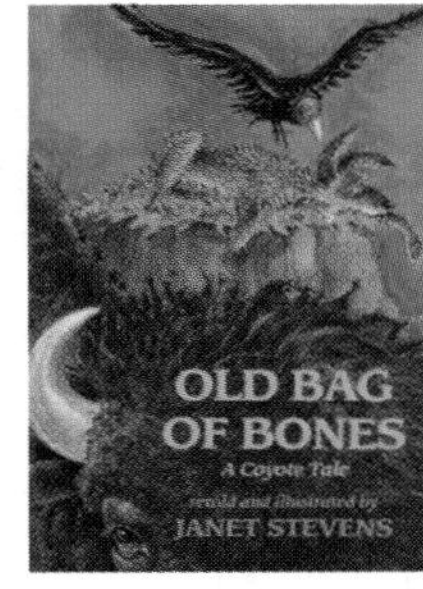

Old Bag of Bones by Janet Stevens. Holiday House, 1997. FOLKTALE: COYOTE AS TRICKSTER

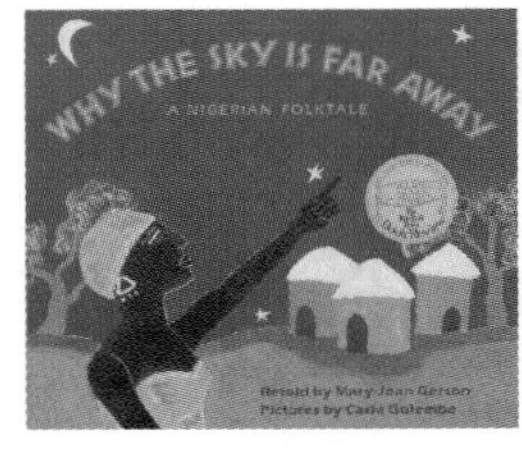

Why the Sky Is Far Away by Mary-Joan Gerson. Little, Brown, 1995. POURQUOI TALE: SKY LORE

Building Background and Concepts

REACHING ALL LEARNERS

ESL

ESL
MANUAL

See *ESL Manual* pages 92–97. You may wish to introduce these additional words and phrases:

place (verb) (page 18)
likenesses (page 19)
handiwork (page 19)
blazed with pride (page 21)
decreed (page 24)

OTHER BACKGROUND-BUILDING IDEAS

VIDEO *Astronomy 101: A Beginner's Guide to the Night Sky.* ©1994 Library Video Company, 25 min.

READ-ALOUD
Anthology

Read-Aloud Anthology, "How the Girl Taught the Coyotes to Sing Harmony," pages 76–77.

INTERNET Bonus Words can be found on *The Learning Site* at **www.harcourtschool.com**

Access Prior Knowledge

Discuss what students know about stars.

Ask students what they know about stars. (Possible response: A star is a glowing object in space, like our sun.) Invite students to name any constellations, or groups of stars, that they know, such as the Big Dipper. Explain that long ago, people made up folktales about how constellations were formed.

Develop Concepts

Build a web using vocabulary words.

Have students create a web about stories that people long ago might have made up about the constellations. Ask questions like these to encourage them to use vocabulary in the web: **Could the stars have been *arranged* by an artist? Would someone need to be *skillful* to form the constellations?** Highlight indicates vocabulary.

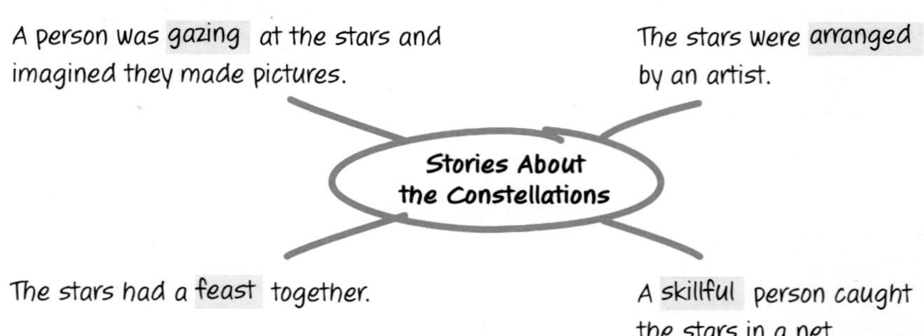
A person was gazing at the stars and imagined they made pictures.
The stars were arranged by an artist.
Stories About the Constellations
The stars had a feast together.
A skillful person caught the stars in a net.

Explain that "Coyote Places the Stars" is a story that was told to explain how the constellations might have come to be.

BONUS WORDS

Introduce action words. If necessary, introduce the following action words found in "Coyote Places the Stars": *bounded, soared, waddled, yelped.*

bounded
soared
waddled
yelped

Introducing Vocabulary

Build Word Identification Strategies

Use structural cues. Display Teaching Transparency 1, and invite volunteers to read the paragraph aloud. Remind students that they can sometimes find familiar word parts in unfamiliar words. Model using this strategy to decode the word *skillful*:

MODEL **When I read *skillful*, I recognize a word in the first syllable—*skill*. I also recognize the suffix *-ful*, which usually means "full of." So someone who is *skillful* must have a lot of skill.**

Have students use familiar word parts and patterns to decode the other vocabulary. Encourage them to confirm their pronunciations by asking themselves: **Does it sound right? Does it make sense?**

CHECK UNDERSTANDING

Practice other vocabulary strategies. Have students answer questions with sentences that show what the vocabulary words mean. MEANINGFUL SENTENCES

- **What part could a river play in making a canyon?** EXPLANATION
- **What word means the opposite of *swiftly*?** ANTONYM
- **What are some things that have been arranged in our classroom?** EXAMPLE
- **What word means the same thing as *gazing*?** SYNONYM
- **What word is in the same word family as *proud*?** RELATED WORDS
- **What would you bring if you were helping put on a feast?** EXAMPLE
- **If you say that a skater is skillful, what do you mean?** DEFINITION

QUICKWRITE

READING NOTEBOOK Have students write for five minutes about things they take *pride* in. They can make a list of accomplishments and other things they are proud of about themselves, such as a scouting award or being a good sport.

VOCABULARY DEFINED

canyon a narrow valley with steep sides

pride a feeling of happiness and satisfaction about doing something well

swiftly very quickly

skillful showing skill; showing a talent for doing something well

feast a special celebration with a large amount of food

gazing looking with a long, steady stare

arranged put in some kind of order

VOCABULARY

Happily, Len watched the moon rise above the deep, dark **canyon**. He was still filled with **pride**. He had caught three rabbits on the hunt that day. Although the rabbits had run **swiftly**, they had not been fast enough to escape his arrows. His father had said he was becoming a **skillful** hunter. Now he was also filled with food, because the village had celebrated the good hunt with a **feast**. Now he lay on his back, **gazing** up at the stars. He saw that one group seemed to be **arranged** in the shape of a rabbit. He began making up a story about a hunter who chased a rabbit into the sky.

▲ Teaching Transparency 1

Name ______________

Coyote Places the Stars — Vocabulary

▶ Complete the sentences with words from the stars.

canyon · skillful · arranged · swiftly · gazing · pride · feast

1. We prepared a __feast__ at our campsite tonight.
2. Later, our __skillful__ cook made a delicious dessert for us.
3. After dinner we all sat around __gazing__ up at the stars.
4. Some stars seemed to be __arranged__ in patterns.
5. After stargazing, we walked to the edge of the __canyon__.
6. We looked down at the __swiftly__ moving river.
7. I took great __pride__ in having chosen such a beautiful place for our camping trip.

▶ Write the words from the stars that match the definitions below.

8. taking a long look at something __gazing__
9. able to do something very well __skillful__
10. celebration with lots of food __feast__

SCHOOL-HOME CONNECTION With your child, discuss sights in nature that you both enjoy. Use at least three of the Vocabulary Words in your discussion.

Journeys of Wonder 3

▲ Practice Book, page 3

SKILL TRACE	
INTRODUCE	
• Before Reading:	T20–T21
• During Reading:	T26, T32
• After Reading:	T40–T41
Reteach	R2
Review 1	T75
Review 2	T119
Test	Theme 1
Maintain	T269

OBJECTIVE:
To understand that time-order words signal sequence of events in stories

BEFORE READING

Preview the Literature

Preview the selection and discuss the genre.

Have students look at the illustrations on pages 14–17 and tell who the main character is. (Coyote) After they have silently read page 17, ask: **Does this story seem to be about something that really happened?**

Prompt students to recall that many stories with talking animals are folktales. Tell them that certain folktales, called *pourquoi* (pôr•kwä´) *tales*, try to explain how something in the natural world might have come to be.

Introduce the Skill

Discuss sequence.

Tell students that recognizing the order in which things happen in a story, or the **sequence** of events, is important to understanding what they are reading. Display Transparency 2, or copy it on the board, and ask volunteers to read it aloud. Then read the example story aloud, and have students explain how the underlined words helped them understand the sequence of events.

SEQUENCE

Sequence is the order in which events happen. The following kinds of words can be clues to sequence.

Time-Order Words	Other Time Words	Dates
first next then finally	morning yesterday Saturday April winter	August 10, 1990 1920s

EXAMPLE:

Long ago there were no stars in the sky, so Turtle carefully opened her jar of stars. First, she used seven stars to make a dipper. Next, she placed the morning star. Finally, she set three together to look like cooking stones.

Coyote could not stop thinking about the sparkling stars. The next night, he crept to the jar. "I will just take a little peek," he said. As soon as he lifted the lid, star after star burst out. The stars scattered across the sky. That is why we see so many stars at night.

Look for time-order words to help you understand the sequence of events. Sometimes it is helpful to add time-order words yourself as you read.

▲ Teaching Transparency 2

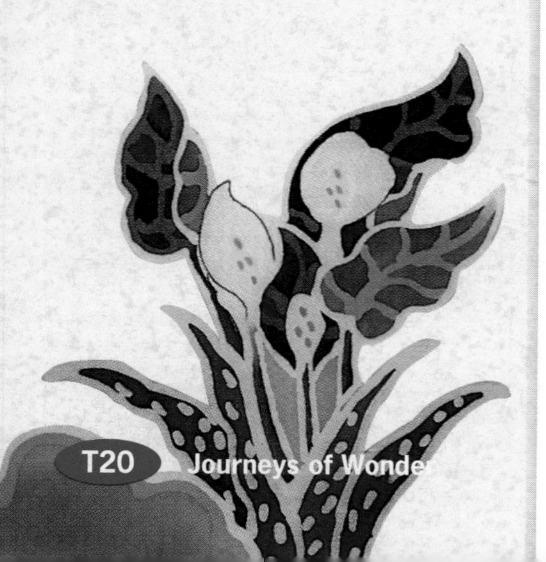

Model the Thinking

Model identifying sequence.

Read aloud and discuss with students the Reading Tip on Teaching Transparency 2. Then use the final paragraph on *Student Edition* page 17 to model identifying the sequence of events.

MODEL **When I begin reading the last paragraph, I see the word *then*. I realize that the author is telling what Coyote did after making the ladder: he climbed it. As I read on, I come to the word *finally*. This word signals that the author is telling the final event: Coyote reached the moon.**

DURING/AFTER READING

- Apply the Skill, pages T26, T32
- Practice the Skill, pages T40–T41

STRATEGY REMINDER

FOCUS STRATEGY Self-Question

Encourage students to monitor their comprehension.

Remind students that they can help themselves understand what they read by asking and answering their own questions. Ask volunteers to explain how asking themselves questions can be helpful. (Possible response: It can help you think about what is happening and why.)

- Apply the Strategy, pages T26, T32

STRATEGIES GOOD READERS USE

- Use Prior Knowledge
- Make and Confirm Predictions
- Adjust Reading Rate
- **Self-Question** FOCUS STRATEGY
- Create Mental Images
- Use Context to Confirm Meaning
- Use Text Structure and Format
- Use Graphic Aids
- Use Reference Sources
- Read Ahead
- Reread
- Summarize

Prereading Strategies

PREVIEW AND PREDICT

Have students read the title, look at the illustrations on pages 14–17, and read page 17. Point out that this is a pourquoi tale, a folktale that tells how something might have come to be. Have students begin a prediction chart for "Coyote Places the Stars." See *Practice Book* page 5.

Prediction Chart	
What I Think Will Happen	What Actually Happens
Coyote will look at the stars and try to move them around.	Coyote builds a ladder and climbs to the moon.

SET PURPOSE

Read to Be Entertained Have students set a purpose for reading "Coyote Places the Stars." Remind them that one purpose for reading is to enjoy a story. If students have difficulty setting a purpose, offer this guidance:

MODEL **As I previewed this folktale, I learned that Coyote builds a ladder to the moon using a bow and arrow. I think I'll read to find out what he does with his bow and arrow on the moon.**

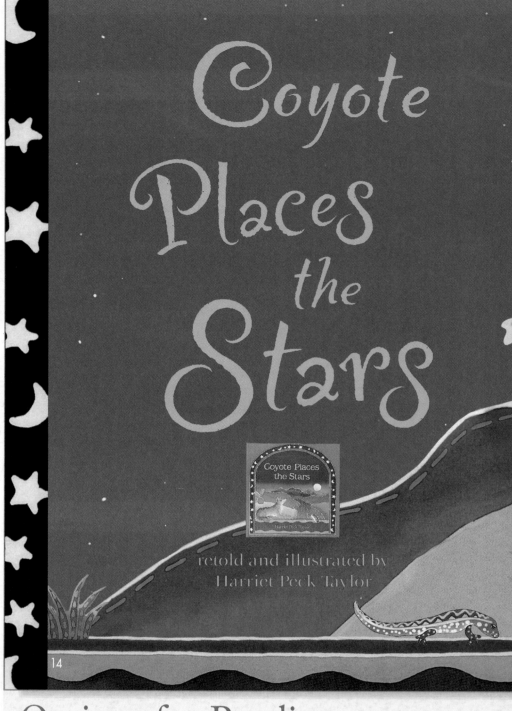

Coyote Places the Stars

retold and illustrated by Harriet Peck Taylor

14

Options for Reading

DIRECTED READING Use the **Monitor Comprehension** questions to check students' comprehension. The **Guided Reading** strategies on pages T24, T26, T28, and T32 provide additional support. WHOLE CLASS/SMALL GROUP

COOPERATIVE READING Have students reading on or above level use *Comprehension Card 4* (page R9) to focus on the **theme.** INDEPENDENT/SMALL GROUP

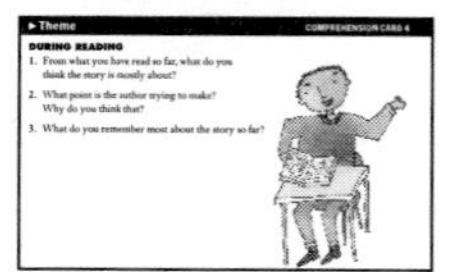

INDEPENDENT READING Have students who are reading on or above level read independently at their own pace. Suggest they make notes in their prediction charts as they read. INDIVIDUAL/WHOLE CLASS

SKILLS IN CONTEXT

Object Pronouns
Review T25

Sequence FOCUS SKILL
Apply T26

Self-Question FOCUS STRATEGY
Apply T26

Homographs and Homophones
Review T27

Vowel Variants: /o͞o/*oo*; /o͝o/*oo, ou*
Review T29

Story Elements
Maintain T31

Sequence FOCUS SKILL
Apply T32

Self-Question FOCUS STRATEGY
Apply T32

Informal Assessment

Individual Reading Inventory T33
Retell T35
Summarize .T35

INTERVENTION STRATEGIES

MODIFIED INSTRUCTION Have students read the title, "Coyote Places the Stars," and tell what they see on the first four pages. Discuss these story words: **heavens, place, handiwork, clever.** Set a purpose for reading to page 19. (to find out what Coyote will do)

EASY READER Students may read "Many Moons Ago," found on pages 126–133 in *New Adventures.* See *New Adventures Intervention Reader Teacher's Guide* pages 92–97.

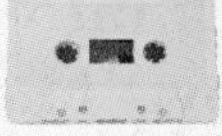

"Coyote Places the Stars" is available on *Literature Cassette 3.*

Monitor Comprehension

1 What clues help you know that the events in this story never really happened? (Possible responses: The animals talk; Coyote can use a bow and arrow; he can shoot an arrow all the way to the moon.) METACOGNITIVE: DISTINGUISH BETWEEN FANTASY AND REALITY

2 What does Coyote's plan to reach the heavens tell you about the kind of character he is? (Possible response: He is curious, ready to try new things, and good at finding solutions to problems.) INFERENTIAL: DETERMINE CHARACTERS' TRAITS

Guided Reading

STRATEGIES GOOD READERS USE

Create Mental Images If students have difficulty understanding how Coyote reached the moon, discuss in a small group how forming a mental picture can help clear up confusion.

MODEL **I wondered how arrows could make a ladder. When I read about the second arrow, I imagined its point stuck into the tail of the first arrow. Then I pictured a long line of arrows stuck together this way.**

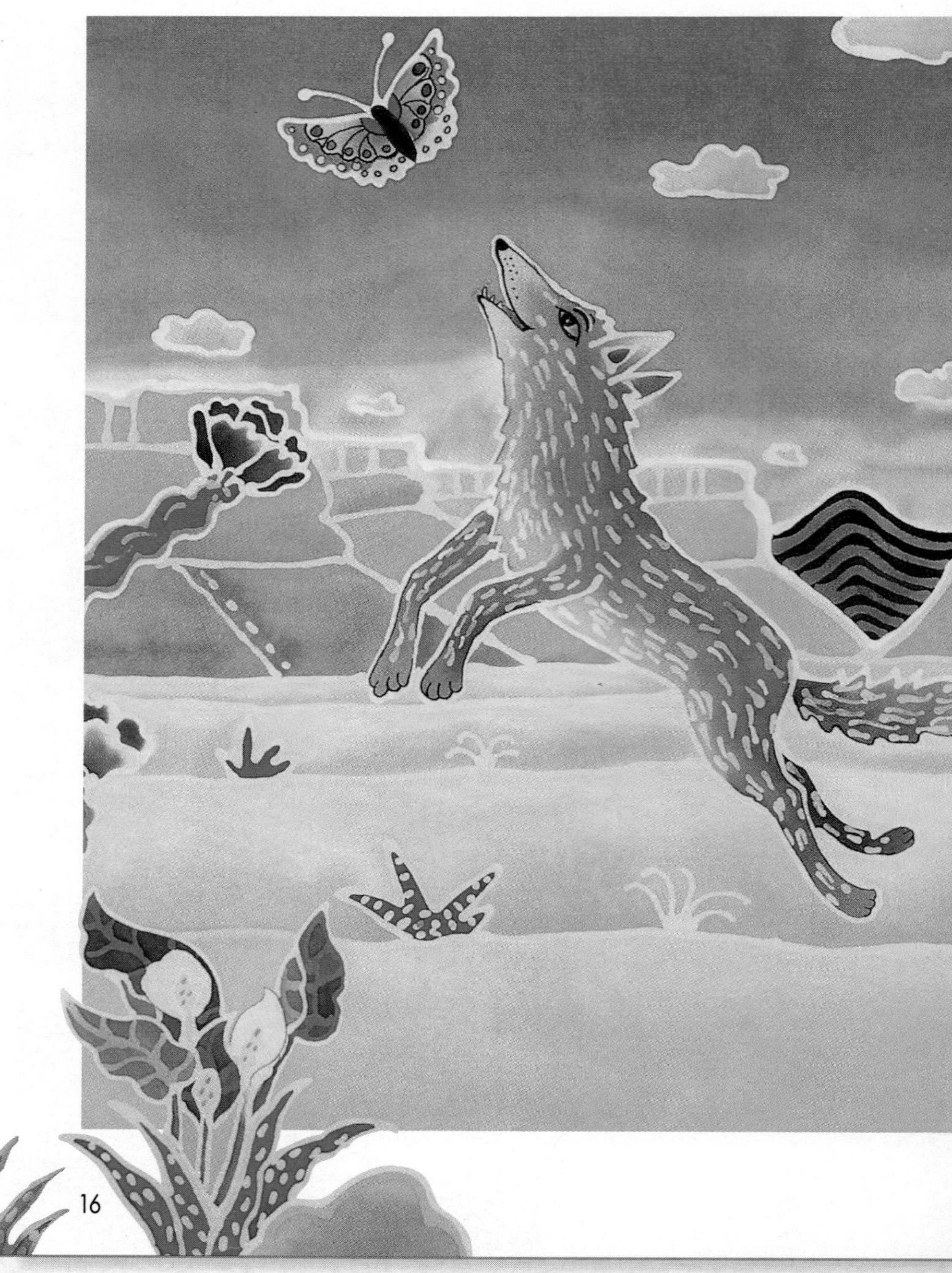

CULTURAL CONNECTIONS

CRAFTY COYOTE Explain that this story is partly based on a Wasco Indian legend. The Wasco live in Oregon. The coyote appears in many Native American tales, mostly because it was admired for its cunning and its ability to survive anywhere. Have students discuss how people in various regions and cultures tell stories about animals with certain traits.

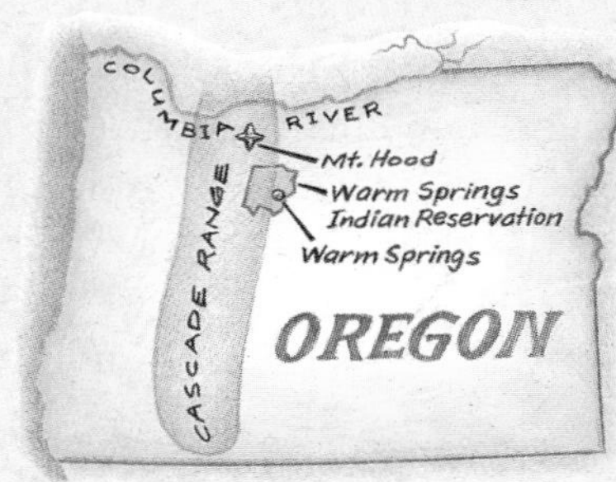

Many moons and many moons ago, a coyote lived in a canyon by a swift-running river. He spent his days roaming the land, chasing butterflies and sniffing wildflowers. He lay awake many nights gazing at the starry heavens.

One summer night, as he was relaxing in the cool grass with his friend Bear, Coyote had an idea. "I think I will climb to the heavens and discover their secrets!"

Bear scratched his big head and asked, "How can you do that?"

"I can get up there with no trouble at all," Coyote said.

Now, Coyote was very skillful with a bow and arrow. He gathered a very large pile of arrows and began to shoot them at the sky. The first arrow whistled through the air and landed on the moon. Coyote launched a second arrow, which caught in the notch of the first. *Whi-rr* went one arrow. *Whizz* went the next, and on and on until this long line of arrows made a ladder.

Coyote then began to climb. He climbed for many days and nights until he finally reached the moon. He slept all that day, as he was very tired.

SKILLS IN CONTEXT

GRAMMAR

SKILL TRACE	
Introduce	T740, 3-1
Review	T25

Object Pronouns

TEACH/MODEL

Have students read the first two sentences in the fifth paragraph on page 17. Ask them to identify the object pronoun. (*them*) Ask who or what this pronoun stands for. (arrows) Model identifying an object pronoun.

MODEL **I know an object pronoun is used after an action verb or after a word such as *above, at, for, from,* or *with.* In the second sentence, *them* follows the action verb *shoot.* So I know that it is an object pronoun.**

PRACTICE/APPLY

Ask students to identify the object pronoun and who or what it stands for in each of these sentences:

1. Coyote gazed at the stars and thought about them. (*them*—stars)
2. Coyote saw Bear and told him about his plan. (*him*—Bear)
3. "Climbing to the heavens is easy for me," said Coyote. (*me*—Coyote)

CHALLENGE

WORD ORIGINS Inform students that many tales use the word *moons* for *months.* Have students suggest why. (The moon completes its cycle—new moon to full moon and back again—every 29½ days.) Have students look at a simple dictionary etymology to see how the word for "moon" became *month* in English. Share with students that they can also see the connection in words from some other languages. (German *Mond*)

Monitor Comprehension

TEKS 3.1C, TEKS 3.3C

1. **When does Coyote discover he can place the stars in patterns?** (after he has climbed to the moon and shot an arrow at a star) TAAS SKILL INFERENTIAL: SEQUENCE

2. **Why does Coyote howl?** (Possible responses: He is pleased with his work; he wants his friends to come see what he has done.) INFERENTIAL: CAUSE-EFFECT

3. **What has Coyote done so far? Is this what you predicted he would do?** (Possible responses: He has gone to the moon and shot arrows to move stars into pictures of his friends. I predicted he would shoot arrows, but I didn't know he would make pictures.) INFERENTIAL: SUMMARIZE/CONFIRM PREDICTIONS

Guided Reading

STRATEGIES GOOD READERS USE

FOCUS STRATEGY **Self-Question** Have individual students read aloud page 19 through the first sentence of the second paragraph. If students have trouble decoding a long word, model self-questioning:

MODEL **I don't know the word *handiwork*, but I can ask myself if it has word parts I recognize. I see two smaller words, *hand* and *work*. Now I can tell that it might mean "work done by hand."**

That night Coyote had another clever idea. He wondered if he could move the stars around by shooting at them with his remaining arrows. His first arrow hit a star and moved it across the sky. He found he could place the stars wherever he wanted.

Coyote wagged his bushy tail and yelped for joy. He was going to make pictures in the sky for all the world to see.

First he decided to make a coyote, so he shot one arrow after another until the stars were arranged in the shape of a coyote. Next he thought of his friend Bear, and placed the stars in the form of a bear.

18

SCIENCE

DISTANCE PERCEPTION Students should already know that the stars are farther away from earth than they seem in this tale. Inform students that the stars in a constellation are not all at the same distance from earth. Of two stars in a constellation that appear to be near each other, one may be very far away and the other much closer to earth.

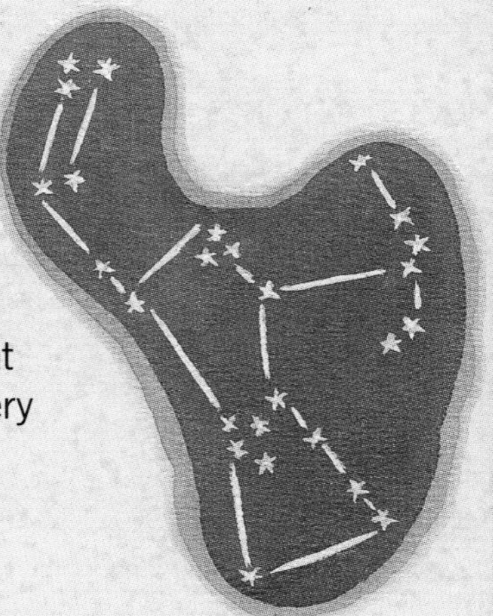

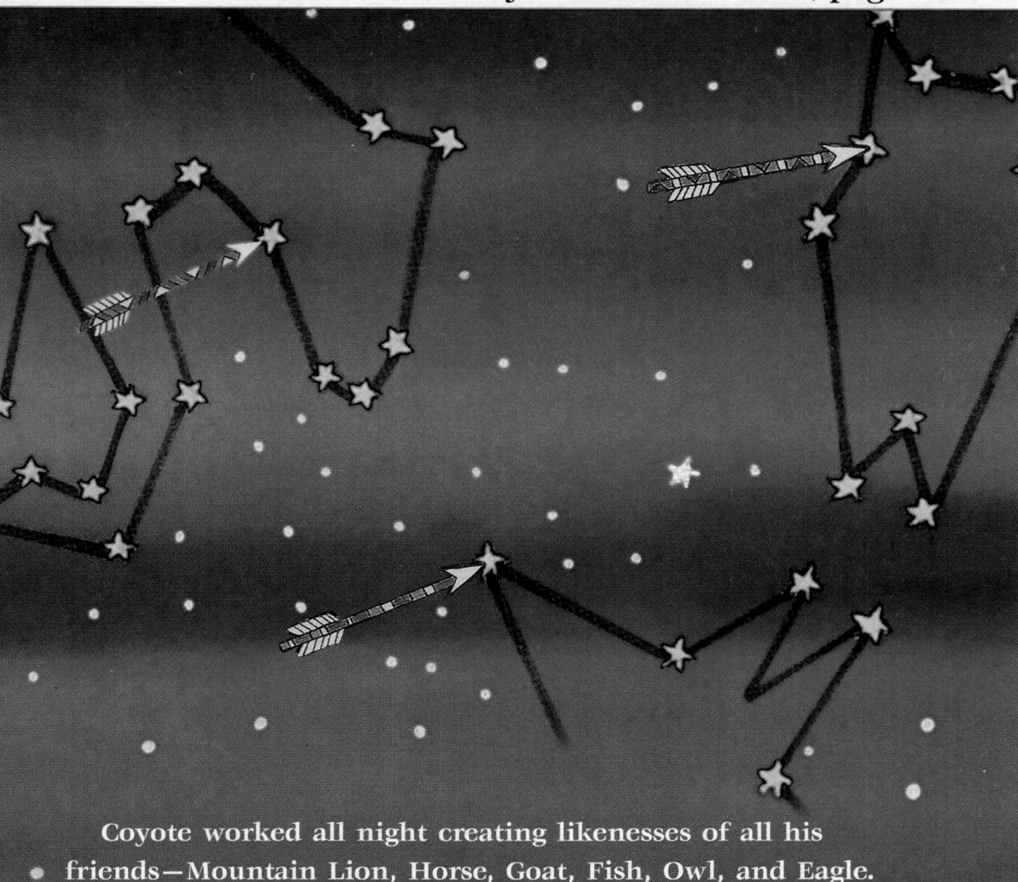

Coyote worked all night creating likenesses of all his friends—Mountain Lion, Horse, Goat, Fish, Owl, and Eagle. With the stars he had left over, he made a Big Road across the sky. When he was finished, he began to descend his ladder back to earth.

That night, when the bright moon rose in the east, Coyote saw his handiwork and began to howl. *Oweowowooooah* was carried on the wind through the shadows of the canyon. Birds and animals awoke suddenly and listened to the mysterious sound. It seemed to be calling to them. From canyons and mesas, hills and plains they came, following the sound.

19

SKILLS IN CONTEXT

VOCABULARY

Homographs and Homophones

SKILL TRACE	
Introduce	T656, T682, 3-1
Reteach	R53, 3-1
Review	T27

TEACH/MODEL

Have students silently reread the second sentence in paragraph 2 on page 19. Ask a volunteer to identify the homograph. (wind) Remind students that *homographs* are words that are spelled the same but are pronounced differently and have different meanings. Next, read aloud the final sentence on page 19. Write *plains* and *planes* on the board, and model using context to determine the meaning of a homophone:

MODEL **_P-l-a-i-n-s_ means "flat land" and _p-l-a-n-e-s_ usually means "airplanes." Since the words _canyons_, _mesas_, and _hills_ all tell about land, I can figure out that _p-l-a-i-n-s_ is being used here.**

PRACTICE/APPLY

Students can read the second paragraph on page 18. Have them write down the homophones (*tail* and *see*) and tell how they knew what meaning each word has.

Name ______________________

Coyote Places the Stars

Homographs and Homophones

Science

Skill Reminder **Homographs:** words that are spelled the same but have different meanings. **Homophones:** words that sound alike but are spelled differently and have different meanings.

▶ Write the correct meaning for the underlined word in each sentence. Choose from the pairs of homographs in the chart.

close: near **close**: to shut	**rose**: a flower **rose**: came up	**light**: not heavy **light**: brightness

1. The sun is bright because it is so close to us. near.
2. We can see the light of the stars when it is dark. brightness.
3. When morning came, the sun rose in the sky came up.

▶ Write the correct word in each sentence. Choose from the pairs of homophones in the chart.

sun: a star **son**: a male child	**bear**: an animal **bare**: empty	**heard**: listened **herd**: a group of animals
tails: parts of animals' bodies **tales**: stories	**knight**: a man given an honor **night**: evening	

4. The sun is the star closest to the earth.
5. People look at the night sky and see groups of stars.
6. People told stories, or tales, about the stars.
7. Other people heard these stories.
8. Some stories were about animals, such as a great bear or a fox.

4 Journeys of Wonder

▲ Practice Book, page 4

INTERVENTION STRATEGIES

MODIFIED INSTRUCTION Help students summarize the story so far: Coyote wants to learn about the heavens, so he makes a ladder with arrows and climbs to the moon. He finds he can place the stars where he wants by shooting arrows at them, so he makes pictures, or likenesses, of his friends. (Make sure students understand that the pictures are not complete outlines.) Coyote goes back and sees his handiwork in the sky. He begins to howl.

Help students set a purpose for reading through page 25. (to find out what happens when the animals follow Coyote's voice)

Monitor Comprehension

1. **Why does Coyote call the other animals to see his work?** (He is proud of his handiwork and wants them to know that he has put their pictures in the sky forever.) CRITICAL: INTERPRET CHARACTERS' MOTIVATIONS

2. **Do you think *parade* is a good word to describe the animals moving toward the sound of Coyote's voice? Why or why not?** (Possible response: yes, because there are a lot of creatures going in one direction at the same time) CRITICAL: AUTHOR'S CRAFT/ INTERPRET IMAGERY

Guided Reading

STRATEGIES GOOD READERS USE

Use Context to Confirm Meaning

Have individual students read aloud the fifth paragraph on page 21. If any student misreads a word, help the student think about the context by asking questions such as:

- **Does what you said make sense?** SEMANTIC CUES
- **Does that word fit there?** SYNTACTIC CUES

AUTHOR'S CRAFT

VIVID VERBS Call attention to the many words on page 21 that tell how the animals move. Point out that the author uses specific words such as *scampered* and *waddled* to help readers imagine the movements of each type of animal. Invite students to list some vivid verbs in a chart and refer to it when writing.

Why say	When you could say...
ran	bounded, scampered, hippety-hopped
flew	soared, glided, zoomed
walked	waddled, crawled, crept

Bears bounded out of their dens. Squirrels scampered and rabbits hippity-hopped over the hills. Bobcats crept and bristly porcupines waddled along the trail.

Graceful deer moved swiftly, while lizards slowly crawled across the desert.

Silvery fish splashed their way upstream. The mighty mountain lion and herds of buffalo joined the journey.

The great eagle soared over moonlit mountains. On and on went the parade of animals, following Coyote's magical voice.

Finally Coyote appeared, high on a rock. The animals formed a huge circle and all became quiet. Coyote's eyes blazed with pride as he said, "Animals and birds and all who are gathered here: Please look at the sky. You will see the stars are arranged in the shapes of animals. I made a ladder to the moon, and from there I shot my arrows to create the pictures you see."

As the animals looked up, a great chorus of whoofing and whiffing, screeching and squawking filled the air.

"I made a coyote and my friend Bear. You will see the mysterious Owl, the great Eagle, the Goat, Horse, Fish, and the mighty Mountain Lion. This is my handiwork, and I hope that all who see it will remember Coyote and all the animals of the canyon."

21

SKILLS IN CONTEXT

DECODING/PHONICS

SKILL TRACE	
Introduce	Grade 2
Review	T29

Vowel Variants: /o͞o/*oo*; /o͝o/*oo*, *ou*

TEACH/MODEL

Write the following sentences from page 21 on the board and have volunteers read them aloud:

Please look at the sky.
I made a ladder to the moon.

Then underline *look* and *moon* and ask students which of these words has the /o͝o/ sound they hear in *could*. (*look*) Remind students that the letters *oo* can stand for the /o͝o/ sound in *look*, or they can stand for the /o͞o/ sound in *moon*. Then remind them that the letter pair *ou* can also stand for the /o͝o/ sound in *could* and *look*.

PRACTICE/APPLY

Write these words on the board: *food, cook, good, should, wood, book, mood, hood*. Have students use rhyming pairs of words to answer these riddles.

1. What do you call an emotion that's making you feel hungry? (a food mood)
2. What do you call a chef who bakes stories? (a book cook)
3. How do you say that a tree trunk ought to do something? (the wood should)

TECHNOLOGY
***PHONICS EXPRESS™* CD-ROM Level D Scooter/Route 1/Harbor and Market**
- ***Phonics Practice Book*, Intermediate, pages 150, 165**
- ***Phonics Practice Reader* 21**

ESL

FIGURATIVE LANGUAGE Point out the clause *Coyote's eyes blazed with pride* on page 21. Explain that a *blaze* is a fire, and *to blaze* is to flash brightly like a flame. Explain that when the author says that Coyote's eyes blazed, she means that his eyes were shining with pride and excitement.

Monitor Comprehension

1 How do you think the animals feel about seeing their pictures in the sky? Why do you think this? (Possible response: They are pleased; they seem to be smiling; I would like it if someone made a picture of me.) INFERENTIAL: DETERMINE CHARACTERS' EMOTIONS

2 How do you know that the author and illustrator feels this is an important moment in the story? (Possible response: She uses two whole pages to show this event.) METACOGNITIVE: AUTHOR'S CRAFT

ART

BATIK The word *batik* means "wax painting" in the Malay language. You might use the description below to explain the process to students.

1. The artist makes a design by putting hot wax onto cloth.

2. The cloth is dipped in dye. The waxed areas do not absorb it.

3. The artist repeats steps one and two with a second color.

SKILLS IN CONTEXT

LITERARY CONCEPTS
TESTED SKILL

Story Elements

SKILL TRACE	
Introduce	T274, T302, 3-1
Reteach	R26, 3-1
Review 1	T329, 3-1
Review 2	T465, 3-1,
Test	Theme 2, 3-1
Maintain	T31

TEACH/MODEL

Ask students who the main character in this story is. (Coyote) Also ask them to describe what is happening. (Possible response: Coyote makes a ladder to the moon. He climbs it and moves the stars around to make pictures. He invites his friends to see the pictures.) Remind students that thinking about how characters, plot, and setting work together can help them understand and enjoy the story. Model identifying setting and noting how setting and plot work together in a story.

MODEL **The author says this story takes place long ago in a canyon by a river. This is the story's setting—the time and place in which the events happen. It makes sense that in a story about how something came to be, the setting would be long ago.**

PRACTICE/APPLY

Have students suggest how the characters might be different if the story took place in a big city in modern times.

REACHING ALL LEARNERS

ESL

This illustration can be used in a variety of ways with ESL students to clarify concepts, facilitate retelling, and reinforce vocabulary. Students at early stages of English acquisition can demonstrate comprehension as they respond to simple questions by pointing. (For example, "Which star picture shows Bear?") More advanced students can tell about the picture or create dialogue between the characters referring to what is happening in the story.

Monitor Comprehension

1 When does the animals' great feast take place? (after they see that Coyote has placed their likenesses in the sky) FOCUS SKILL INFERENTIAL: SEQUENCE

2 Do you think Coyote expected the other animals to react the way they did? Explain. (Possible response: No, because if he was expecting them to be so pleased, he would not be so grateful.) INFERENTIAL: DETERMINE CHARACTERS' EMOTIONS

Guided Reading

STRATEGIES GOOD READERS USE

FOCUS STRATEGY **Self-Question** If students are not sure why Coyote was so grateful, they may not have thought about what he expected to happen. You may want to model self-questioning:

MODEL **I wondered why Coyote promised to be their friend forever. I asked myself, "Why would anyone feel like that?" Then I realized that Coyote was probably very surprised, because he hadn't expected the other animals to make such a fuss.**

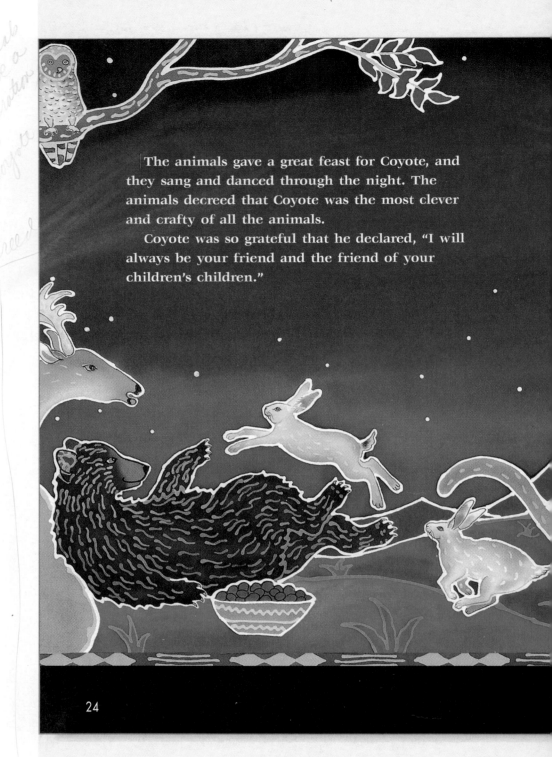

The animals gave a great feast for Coyote, and they sang and danced through the night. The animals decreed that Coyote was the most clever and crafty of all the animals.

Coyote was so grateful that he declared, "I will always be your friend and the friend of your children's children."

24

WORD STUDY

SYNONYMS Point out the word *decreed* on page 24. Ask a volunteer what this word means here. ("announced their decision") Explain that this word is usually used to tell about an announcement of a new law made by a powerful ruler. Have students make a web of other words the author could have used instead of *decreed* and then judge whether *decreed* was the best choice.

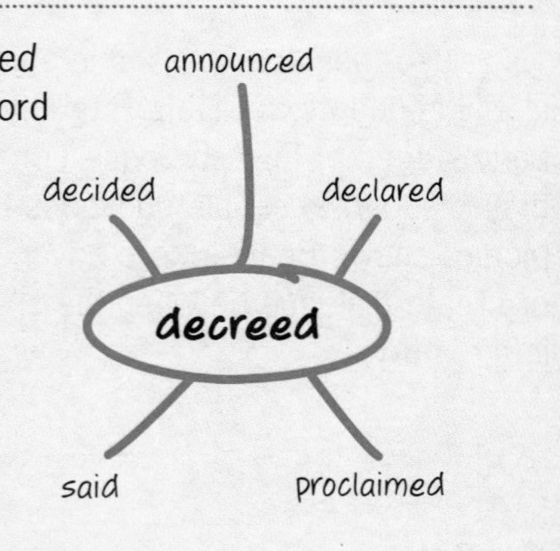

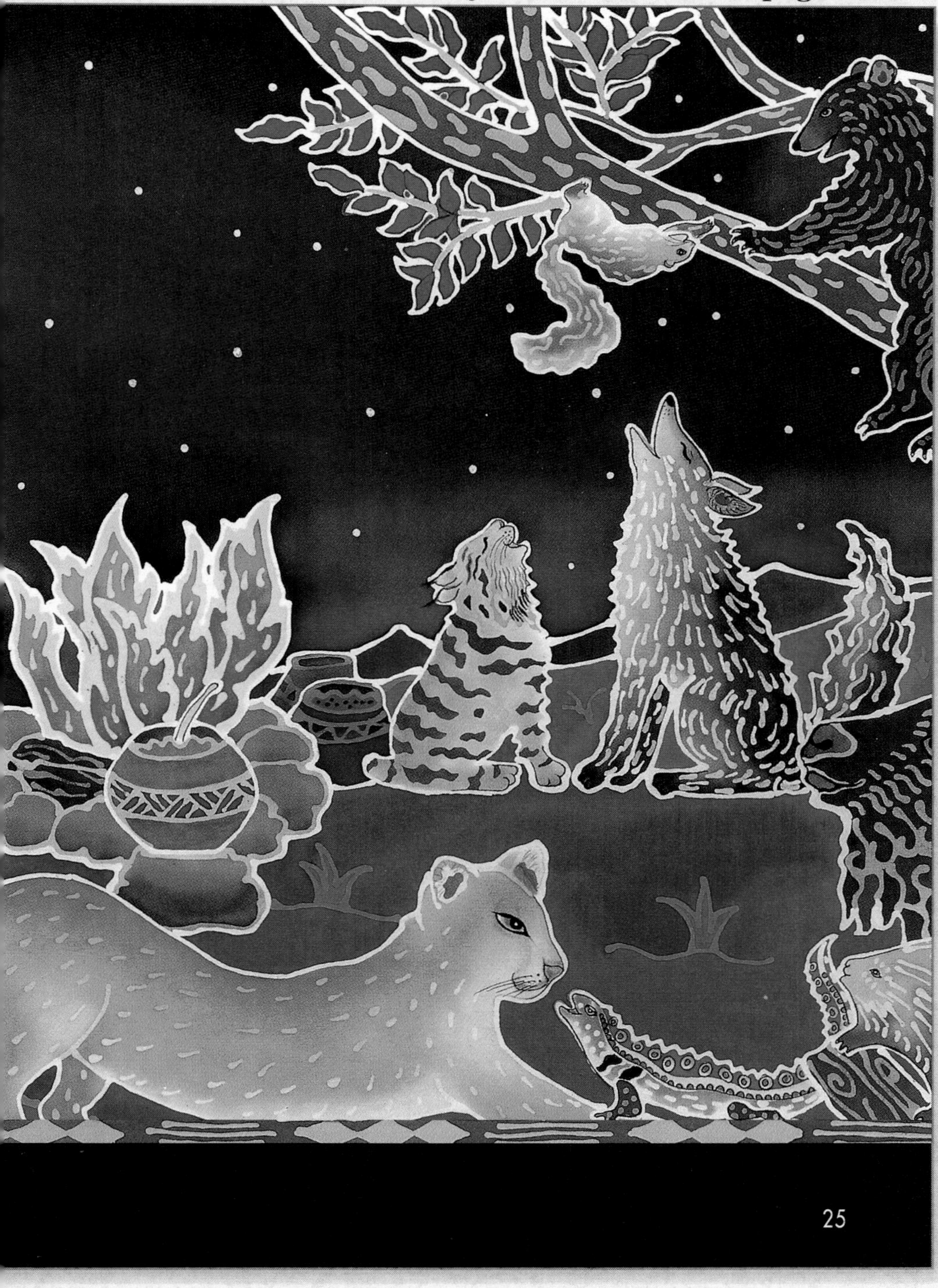

Coyote Places the Stars, pages 24–25

Informal Assessment

INDIVIDUAL READING INVENTORY

Have students read aloud the bracketed passage on pages 24–26. For this passage, you may want to focus on the following:

Number of words read: 97

Number of meaning-based miscues: ______

Number of symbol/sound miscues: ______

Number of self-corrections: ______

A complete guide to keeping and interpreting individual reading inventories, including recording forms to monitor students' progress throughout the year, appears on pages R99–R107.

REACHING ALL LEARNERS

INTERVENTION STRATEGIES

MODIFIED INSTRUCTION Help students summarize the animals' reactions. The animals are happy to see the pictures in the sky. They give a feast for Coyote and say he is <u>clever</u>. Coyote is grateful and promises to always be their friend. Then summarize the whole story:

- Coyote climbs to the moon to learn more about the heavens.
- He makes pictures of his friends by shooting arrows at the stars.
- When the animals see their pictures, they thank Coyote with a feast.

Discuss the idea that this story tells how someone imagined the constellations came to be.

Literary Response

RETURN TO THE PREDICTIONS/PURPOSE

What did you predict Coyote would do in "Coyote Places the Stars"? Did your predictions turn out to be correct? Ask students whether their purposes for reading were met.

APPRECIATING THE LITERATURE

Do you think Harriet Peck Taylor is a good storyteller? Give examples from the story to explain your answer. (Responses will vary. Students should support their opinions.)

Think About It

1. **What did Coyote do to the stars in the night sky? Why did he do this?** (He shot arrows at them and moved them into patterns. He wanted everyone who saw the star pictures to remember the animals of the canyon.) INFERENTIAL: SUMMARIZE

2. **What pictures would you have drawn with the stars?** (Responses will vary.) CRITICAL: PERSONAL RESPONSE

3. **How does this story explain why Coyote howls?** (It says he is calling for everyone to gaze at the stars and dream.) CRITICAL: LITERARY ANALYSIS/THEME CONNECTION

Now, to this day, if you listen closely in the still of the night as the moon is rising, you may even hear the magical howl of Coyote. He is calling you to go to your window, to gaze at the star pictures, and to dream.]

Think About It

1. What did Coyote do to the stars in the night sky? Why did he do this?
2. What pictures would you have drawn with the stars?
3. How does this story explain why Coyote howls?

26

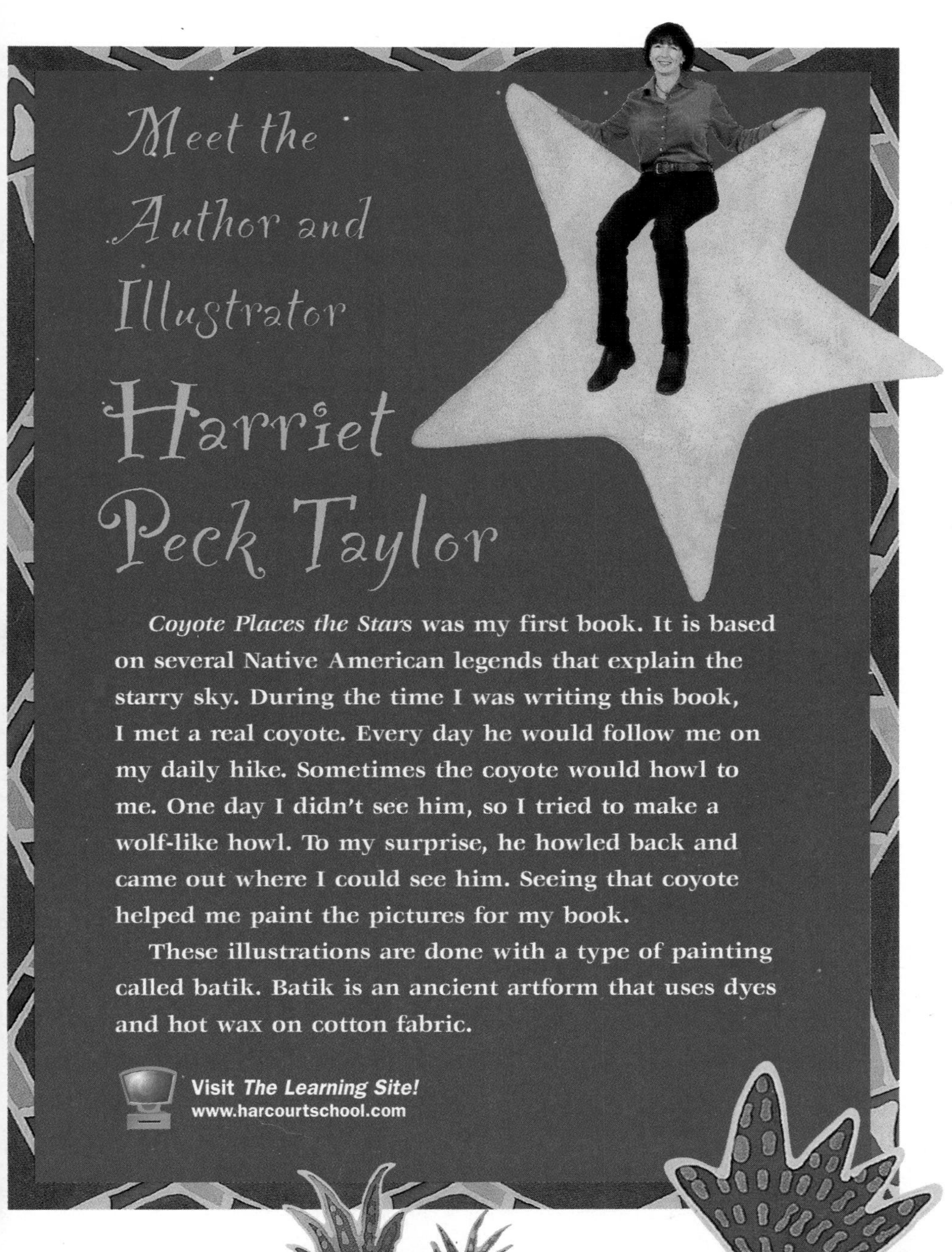

Meet the Author and Illustrator Harriet Peck Taylor

Coyote Places the Stars was my first book. It is based on several Native American legends that explain the starry sky. During the time I was writing this book, I met a real coyote. Every day he would follow me on my daily hike. Sometimes the coyote would howl to me. One day I didn't see him, so I tried to make a wolf-like howl. To my surprise, he howled back and came out where I could see him. Seeing that coyote helped me paint the pictures for my book.

These illustrations are done with a type of painting called batik. Batik is an ancient artform that uses dyes and hot wax on cotton fabric.

Visit *The Learning Site!*
www.harcourtschool.com

ABOUT THE AUTHOR AND ILLUSTRATOR

HARRIET PECK TAYLOR says her art has become more imaginative over the years. "My work reflects a playful approach to the world around me. Bears dance under a moonlit sky and fish may fly. . . . They call out to the child who is in all of us."

Ask students how they think Taylor's experience with the real coyote might have helped her write and illustrate "Coyote Places the Stars." (Possible response: Seeing a real coyote might have helped her know how coyotes look and act.)

INTERNET Additional author information can be found on *The Learning Site* at **www.harcourtschool.com**

Informal Assessment

RETELL

Have each student retell the story. Monitor whether the student

- ☐ relates the main events in sequence.
- ☐ provides important supporting details.
- ☐ includes the story elements: the main character, the setting, what the character does, and how he does it.
- ☐ identifies the story as a pourquoi tale.

SUMMARIZE

Encourage students to summarize "Coyote Places the Stars." Suggest that they complete and then refer to the prediction chart they began before reading. See *Practice Book* page 5.

ONE-SENTENCE SUMMARY Have students use their completed prediction charts to write a one-sentence summary of "Coyote Places the Stars."

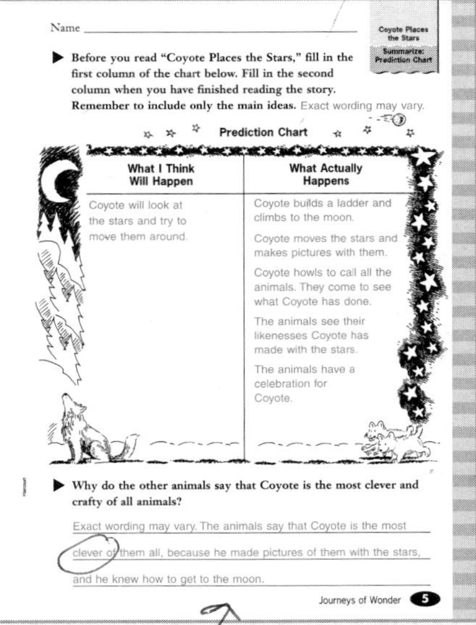

Name ______________________

Coyote Places the Stars
Summarize: Prediction Chart

▶ **Before you read "Coyote Places the Stars," fill in the first column of the chart below. Fill in the second column when you have finished reading the story. Remember to include only the main ideas.** Exact wording may vary.

Prediction Chart

What I Think Will Happen	What Actually Happens
Coyote will look at the stars and try to move them around.	Coyote builds a ladder and climbs to the moon. Coyote moves the stars and makes pictures with them. Coyote howls to call all the animals. They come to see what Coyote has done. The animals see their likenesses Coyote has made with the stars. The animals have a celebration for Coyote.

▶ **Why do the other animals say that Coyote is the most clever and crafty of all animals?**

Exact wording may vary. The animals say that Coyote is the most clever of them all, because he made pictures of them with the stars, and he knew how to get to the moon.

Journeys of Wonder 5

▲ **Practice Book, page 5**

Activity Choices

MEET ME AT THE ROCK

Write an Announcement Read aloud to students ads and fliers for upcoming events, and have them listen to distinguish and evaluate reasons, facts, and opinions. Remind students to include reasons in their announcements. CRITICAL: REFLECT INTERPRETATIONS

STAR PICTURES

Draw a Constellation Allow students time to examine a map of the constellations. Offer help with pronunciation of constellation names. Display completed drawings in the classroom or the school hallway. CREATIVE: ART

FESTIVAL OF STARS

Write a Song Explain that songs are sometimes poems put to music. Students can take turns reading aloud to their partners the lyrics they've written to identify musical elements. Have them point out to you the rhymes and repeated sounds. CREATIVE: MUSIC

THANKS, COYOTE!

Write a Letter Small groups might begin by brainstorming reasons that the star pictures are a good idea. Review with students the correct form for a friendly letter before they begin writing. CRITICAL: SUPPORT INTERPRETATIONS

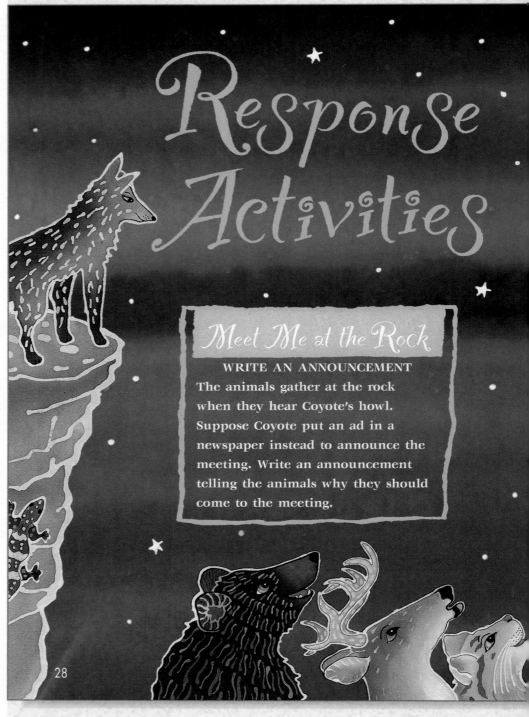

Response Activities

Meet Me at the Rock

WRITE AN ANNOUNCEMENT

The animals gather at the rock when they hear Coyote's howl. Suppose Coyote put an ad in a newspaper instead to announce the meeting. Write an announcement telling the animals why they should come to the meeting.

28

SCHOOL-HOME CONNECTION

Encourage students to work together with their families to complete the activities on the copying master on page R18. You may assign some or all of the activities as homework during the week.

TEST TUTOR Family members can help students prepare for standardized or state tests on *The Learning Site* at: **www.harcourtschool.com**

Copying Master, p. R18 ▶

School–Home Connection

Your child is reading "Coyote Places the Stars" by Harriet Peck Taylor. This story is adapted from several Native American folktales that tell a story about why we see constellations in the sky. You and your child may enjoy sharing the story and these activities. As you do so, you will be helping your child develop language skills.

Traditional Tales

Help your child read and discuss other traditional tales. Look for books like these in your local library:

- *Why the Sky Is Far Away* by Mary-Joan Gerson. Little, Brown, 1995.
- *Anansi and the Talking Melon* by Eric A. Kimmel. Holiday House, 1995.
- *Coyote Steals the Blanket* by Janet Stevens. Holiday House, 1993.

VOCABULARY

What Word Is It?

The following words are new vocabulary your child has learned while reading "Coyote Places the Stars":

canyon	swiftly
gazing	pride
skillful	feast
arranged	

You might enjoy playing a guessing game with your child to reinforce the meanings of these words. (Example: "I'm thinking of a word for a valley with steep walls.")

Listen to a Storyteller

Today, as in past years, storytellers keep traditions alive by telling old stories to new generations. Your family can be a part of this process. With your child, attend a storyteller's performance in your community. Afterward, work with your child to retell the storyteller's best story to others in your family. Encourage your child to write down that story or a story of his or her own.

R18 Coyote Places the Stars Visit The Learning Site! School-Home Connection

Star Pictures

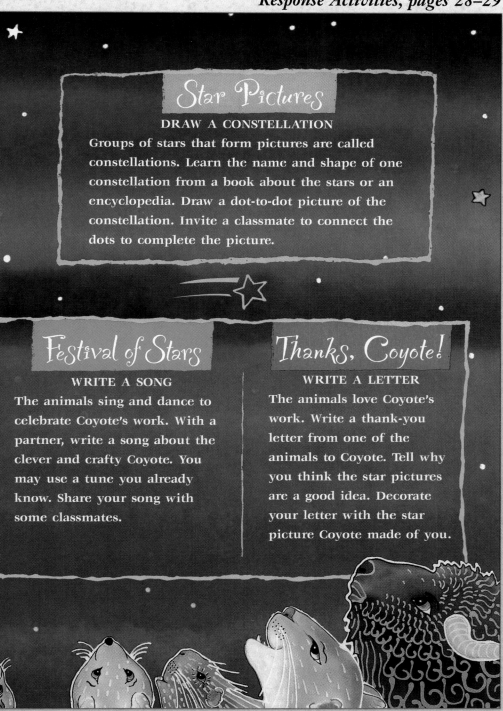

DRAW A CONSTELLATION

Groups of stars that form pictures are called constellations. Learn the name and shape of one constellation from a book about the stars or an encyclopedia. Draw a dot-to-dot picture of the constellation. Invite a classmate to connect the dots to complete the picture.

Festival of Stars

WRITE A SONG

The animals sing and dance to celebrate Coyote's work. With a partner, write a song about the clever and crafty Coyote. You may use a tune you already know. Share your song with some classmates.

Thanks, Coyote!

WRITE A LETTER

The animals love Coyote's work. Write a thank-you letter from one of the animals to Coyote. Tell why you think the star pictures are a good idea. Decorate your letter with the star picture Coyote made of you.

Assessment

SELECTION COMPREHENSION TEST

To evaluate comprehension, see pages 1–3.

INFORMAL ASSESSMENT

PERFORMANCE ASSESSMENT The letter students completed for Thanks, Coyote! may be used for performance assessment of story comprehension.

PORTFOLIO OPPORTUNITY

Students may want to add their announcements from Meet Me at the Rock to their portfolios.

REACHING ALL LEARNERS

INTERVENTION STRATEGIES

SONG LYRICS Some students may need help writing song lyrics for the Festival of Stars activity. Guide these students to think of rhymes for *bear, star, sky, see, drew,* and other words they may want to use. Then model constructing simple pairs of rhyming lines:

> MODEL **I know that *you* rhymes with *drew*. I'm going to pretend I'm Bear and try to make up two lines of a song I could sing to another animal: *In the sky, Coyote drew/a picture of me and a picture of you.***

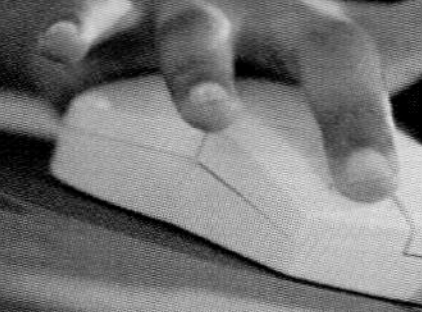

Building Literacy Skills

REREADING FOR FLUENCY

Record a Story

Have groups of students practice and record a reading of "Coyote Places the Stars" for the classroom library. Some students can read dialogue, some group members can take turns reading the narrative, and others can provide sound effects. Remind students to practice rereading until they can read fluently, to use expression, and to pay attention to punctuation. SPEAKING/READING

WRITING

Sequence of Instructions

Have students role-play Coyote teaching other animals how to move stars to make pictures. Have students list the steps in the process on large chart paper, beginning with shooting one arrow into the moon. Then have them read aloud the directions to a small group, pointing to each step on their charts. Listeners should practice responding appropriately to directions. LISTENING/SPEAKING/WRITING

ORAL LANGUAGE

Tell a Round-Robin Tale

Suggest that students work in groups to tell a round-robin tale about some animals like those in the story. Explain that one person is to begin the story by talking for about a minute, and then the next person can pick up the story. Have them refer to the speaking and listening tips on Activity Card 31, page R13, to help them become good storytellers. LISTENING/SPEAKING

Activity Card 31 ▶

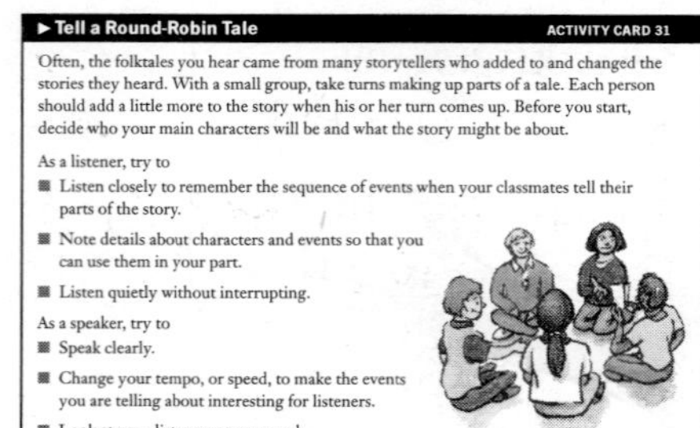

▶ Tell a Round-Robin Tale ACTIVITY CARD 31

Often, the folktales you hear came from many storytellers who added to and changed the stories they heard. With a small group, take turns making up parts of a tale. Each person should add a little more to the story when his or her turn comes up. Before you start, decide who your main characters will be and what the story might be about.

As a listener, try to

- Listen closely to remember the sequence of events when your classmates tell their parts of the story.
- Note details about characters and events so that you can use them in your part.
- Listen quietly without interrupting.

As a speaker, try to

- Speak clearly.
- Change your tempo, or speed, to make the events you are telling about interesting for listeners.
- Look at your listeners as you speak.

VIEWING

Reflected Light

Have students look at the illustration on pages 18–19 of "Coyote Places the Stars." Point out that some parts of Coyote are lighter than others because light is shining on him. Explain that illustrators show light by using lighter colors for parts of an object that has light shining on it. Have students draw a picture that shows moonlit objects and use lighter colors to show where the light is shining. VIEWING/REPRESENTING

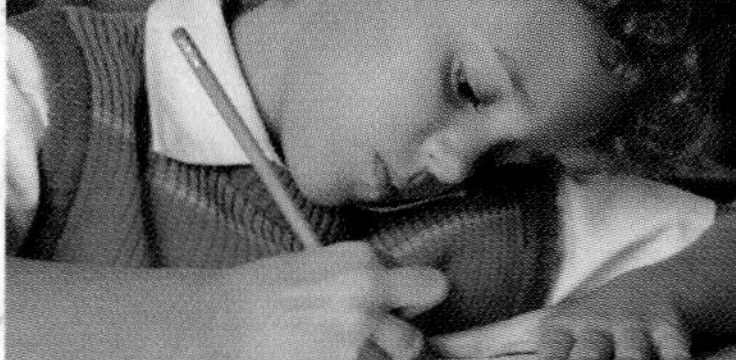

Intervention Strategies for Below-Level Readers

REREADING

Reinforce Comprehension

FOCUS STRATEGY **Apply the focus strategy.** Remind students that using strategies while reading will help them better understand what they read. Have them explain how they used the Self-Question strategy while reading "Coyote Places the Stars." Discuss the strategy by asking questions such as these:

- **Why is it a good idea to stop and ask yourself questions when you read?**
- **What kinds of questions might you ask yourself when you read?**

Encourage students to practice using this strategy as they reread a section of "Coyote Places the Stars." As they silently reread pages 18–21, have them use a chart like the one below to note the questions they asked themselves and the page numbers where they found the answers.

Question	Page	Answer
Why does Coyote first shoot an arrow at a star?	18	He wonders whether he can move the stars around by doing this.
Why do the animals gather together?	21	They follow Coyote's voice.
Why does Coyote feel proud?	21	He has been to the moon and arranged the stars in patterns.

LANGUAGE EXPLORATION

Onomatopoeic Words

Discuss words that represent sounds. In "Coyote Places the Stars," the author uses the words *whirr* and *whizz* to describe the sound of arrows flying through the air (page 17). Tell students that sometimes writers use words that represent sounds. Ask students to name some sound words they know, and begin a web on the board.

Point out to students that other languages also have words like these. Add the following words for a dog's bark to the web, and discuss how they are similar to and different from the English *bow-wow*:

Greek: gar-gar
Russian: how-how
French: wah-wah
Korean: mong-mong

Ask students who speak another language to share some words like this in their language.

AFTER READING

SKILL TRACE	
INTRODUCE	
• Before Reading:	T20–T21
• During Reading:	T26, T32
• After Reading:	T40–T41
Reteach	R2
Review 1	T75
Review 2	T119
Test	Theme 1
Maintain	T269

OBJECTIVE:

To understand that time-order words signal sequence of events in stories

CHALLENGE

Have students read other folktales and find one in which the sequence of events is important. Ask students to explain why this is so.

INTERVENTION

Have students draw a comic strip to show the sequence of events in the first half of "Coyote Places the Stars." Help them talk about the sequence, using time-order words.

RETEACH See page R2 for a lesson in multiple modalities.

Return to the Concept

Extend the thinking. Remind students that paying attention as they read to the order of events makes it easier to understand the important events. Record what they remember about "Coyote Places the Stars" on a chart:

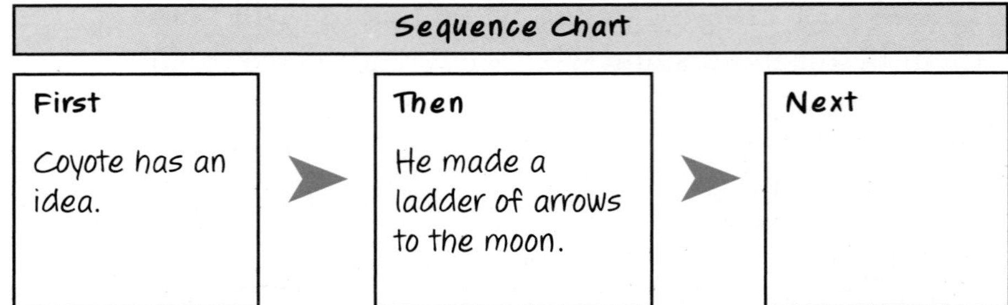

Sequence Chart
First
Coyote has an idea.
Then
He made a ladder of arrows to the moon.
Next

Model thinking about sequence. Have students read page 30 in the *Student Edition*. Ask how words such as *first*, *next*, and *finally* help them understand the sequence of events. You may wish to model the thinking.

MODEL **To understand the order of a story's events, I look for time-order words like *first*, *next*, and *finally*. I know, for example, that *finally* means "last."**

Summarize. Ask students how paying careful attention to the sequence of events helped them understand "Coyote Places the Stars."

Guided Practice

Discuss time-order words. Have students read the passage on page 31. Work with them to create a sequence diagram showing the order of events. Encourage students to make note of the time-order words.

Test Prep

These tips can help students answer sequence test items.

- Pay attention to the order in which the author tells about events.
- Watch for time-order words that give clues.

FOCUS SKILL

Sequence

In "Coyote Places the Stars," Coyote makes plans and carries them out in order. Many stories are told in the order in which the events happen, or in **sequence.** Sometimes authors use time-order words such as **first, next, then, later,** and **finally.** These words let readers know the order in which things happen.

This diagram shows the sequence of events in "Coyote Places the Stars." You can use boxes and arrows like these to help you show when things happen in a story.

First, Coyote builds a ladder of arrows and climbs to the moon. → **Next,** he shoots arrows at the stars to make pictures of his animal friends. → **Then,** Coyote climbs down and calls all the animals to see his pictures in the sky. → **Finally,** the animals celebrate what Coyote has done.

30

When you read a story, think about the order in which things happen. This will help you understand the ideas and events that lead to the ending. Watch for time-order words that give you clues.

Read the story below. What does Coyote do first, next, and last?

Snake was unhappy. "I don't see a star shape that looks like me," he said.

"I can fix that," said Coyote. First, he tied an arrow to a long, strong rope. Next, he shot the arrow into the sky and hooked it to a star. Then, he tugged hard on the rope. As the star tumbled toward Earth, it pulled a tail of fire behind it.

"It looks just like me!" cried Snake.

WHAT HAVE YOU LEARNED?

1. **Reread one of your favorite stories. List some of the time-order words in the story that help you understand the sequence of events.**
2. **What might happen if the story events in "Coyote Places the Stars" were written out of sequence? Explain how this would be confusing.**

Visit *The Learning Site!* www.harcourtschool.com

TRY THIS • TRY THIS • TRY THIS

Think of a favorite game. What are some of the steps for playing this game? Write four steps in order.

To play this game, this is what you do:

1. First,
2. Next,
3. Then,
4. Finally,

31

▲ Student Edition, pages 30–31

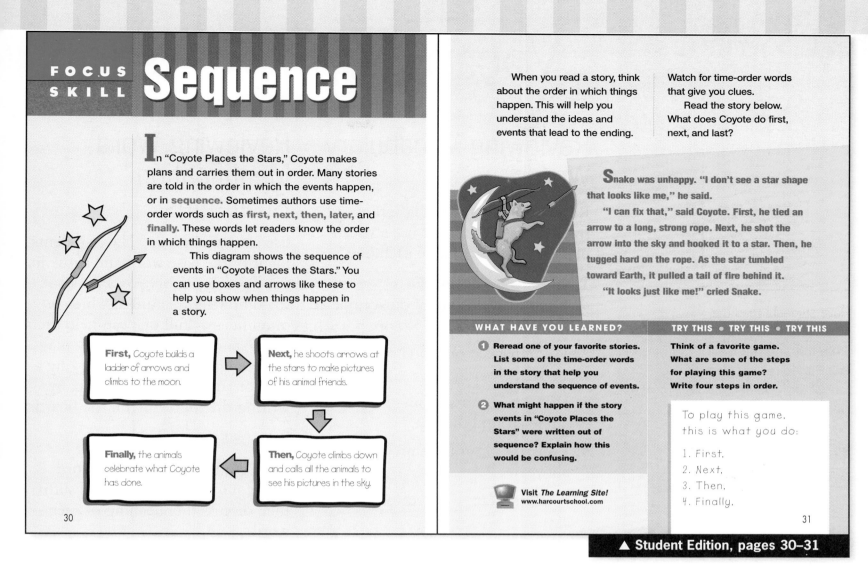

Practice/Apply

Have students apply the skill. Have students answer the questions and complete the activity on page 31.

WHAT HAVE YOU LEARNED?

1. Possible responses: *first, next, finally, before, after, when, until*
2. Possible response: It might be hard to understand what caused the story events to happen if they were out of order. For instance, if the story began with the celebration, we wouldn't understand why the animals were celebrating.

INTERNET Students can use the Sequence Activities on *The Learning Site* at **www.harcourtschool.com**

TRY THIS

Have students think of a game they know and record the steps involved in playing using sequence words. If students want to list more than four steps, suggest that they use *Next* and *Then* more than once.

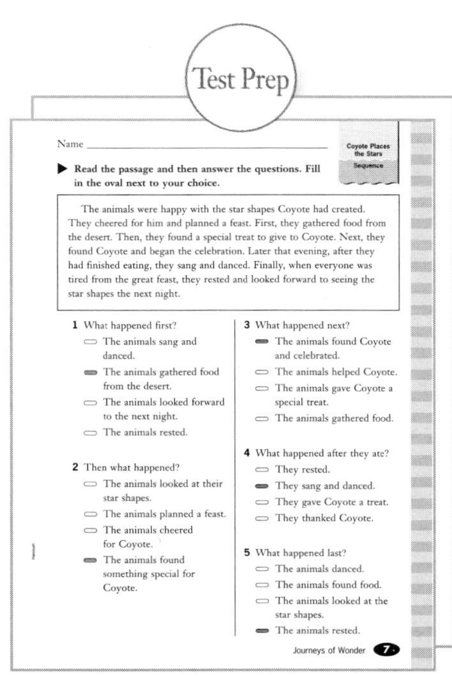

Test Prep

Name ______

Coyote Places the Stars
Sequence

▶ Read the passage and then answer the questions. Fill in the oval next to your choice.

The animals were happy with the star shapes Coyote had created. They cheered for him and planned a feast. First, they gathered food from the desert. Then, they found a special treat to give to Coyote. Next, they found Coyote and began the celebration. Later that evening, after they had finished eating, they sang and danced. Finally, when everyone was tired from the great feast, they rested and looked forward to seeing the star shapes the next night.

1 What happened first?
- The animals sang and danced.
- The animals gathered food from the desert. (filled)
- The animals looked forward to the next night.
- The animals rested.

2 Then what happened?
- The animals looked at their star shapes.
- The animals planned a feast.
- The animals cheered for Coyote.
- The animals found something special for Coyote. (filled)

3 What happened next?
- The animals found Coyote and celebrated. (filled)
- The animals helped Coyote.
- The animals gave Coyote a special treat.
- The animals gathered food.

4 What happened after they ate?
- They rested.
- They sang and danced. (filled)
- They gave Coyote a treat.
- They thanked Coyote.

5 What happened last?
- The animals danced.
- The animals found food.
- The animals looked at the star shapes.
- The animals rested. (filled)

Journeys of Wonder 7

▲ Practice Book, pages 6–7

Vocabulary Workshop

Phaeton and the Chariot of the Sun

by Nathan Patterson
illustrated by Rosiland Solomon

Have students read the **TAKE-HOME BOOK *Phaeton and the Chariot of the Sun*** to reinforce vocabulary words. See also *Guided Reading Manual for Take-Home Books*, page 17.

Reviewing Vocabulary Words

Read aloud the following sentence frames. Have a student use a vocabulary word to complete each one.

1. The steep walls of the _____ rose on either side of our camp. *(canyon)*
2. We unpacked our food and had a _____ . *(feast)*
3. We _____ our sleeping bags in a circle around the fire. *(arranged)*
4. I was _____ at the starry sky above. *(gazing)*
5. A falling star _____ crossed the sky. *(swiftly)*
6. We thought Juan could tell us a wonderful story because he is a _____ storyteller. *(skillful)*
7. Juan smiled with _____ as he began to speak. *(pride)*

Reviewing Word Identification Strategies

Use structural cues. Have students identify the base word and suffix in the word *joyful* (*joy, -ful*). Point out that knowing this suffix, which often means "full of," can help them understand many words they may not recognize. Model identifying a base or root word and a suffix by writing the following on the board:

joy + ful = joyful

Have students divide each word below into its base word and suffix; then discuss the meaning of each word.

respectful	**healthful**
tearful	**powerful**

Cross-Curricular Words Have students search textbooks from other subjects for examples of descriptive words that use suffixes. Guide them to sort the words based on what they describe. (Possible responses: words that describe actions: *carefully, slowly, gently;* words that describe people and places: *beautiful, endless, powerful*)

Extending Vocabulary

IDENTIFY SOUND-ALIKES

Homophones Write the words *bear* and *bare* on the board. Point out that *bear* and *bare* are homophones—they sound the same but have different spellings and meanings.

Homophones
bare/bear

Ask volunteers to add more examples to the list. Possible responses: *see/sea, days/daze, scene/seen*) Have students use the word pairs in sentences that give examples.

Write on the board these words from the story:

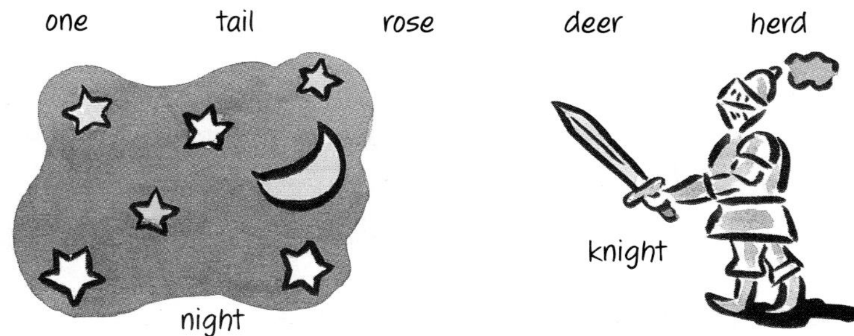

Have students work in pairs to think of a homophone for each word, and then draw sketches to illustrate the meanings of these homophones. (Responses: *won, tale, rows, dear, heard*) Have students use a dictionary to help them find the correct spelling of a homophone.

ANIMAL RIDDLES

Reference Sources/Encyclopedia Recall with students that the author used colorful adjectives for some of the animals in the story. For example, she called the porcupines *bristly* and the fish *silvery*. Have students look up one of the story animals in an encyclopedia to see what adjectives are used for the animal.

Then have students make up adjective riddles about animals. Offer this riddle as an example: I am large, shaggy, and powerful. Who am I? (bear)

ESL

You may want to give students extra practice identifying homophones. Have them copy the following lists of words and draw lines to connect story words with their homophones.

Story Words	Homophones
see	grate
plains	sea
great	here
hear	planes

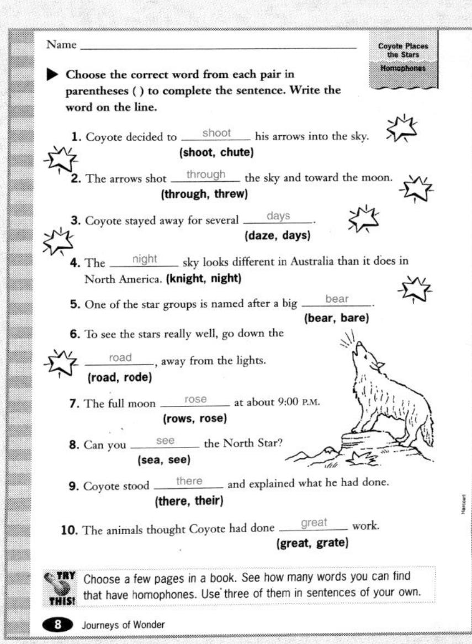

Name ____________

Coyote Places the Stars
Homophones

▶ **Choose the correct word from each pair in parentheses ( ) to complete the sentence. Write the word on the line.**

1. Coyote decided to ___shoot___ his arrows into the sky. **(shoot, chute)**

2. The arrows shot ___through___ the sky and toward the moon. **(through, threw)**

3. Coyote stayed away for several ___days___. **(daze, days)**

4. The ___night___ sky looks different in Australia than it does in North America. **(knight, night)**

5. One of the star groups is named after a big ___bear___. **(bear, bare)**

6. To see the stars really well, go down the ___road___, away from the lights. **(road, rode)**

7. The full moon ___rose___ at about 9:00 P.M. **(rows, rose)**

8. Can you ___see___ the North Star? **(sea, see)**

9. Coyote stood ___there___ and explained what he had done. **(there, their)**

10. The animals thought Coyote had done ___great___ work. **(great, grate)**

TRY THIS! Choose a few pages in a book. See how many words you can find that have homophones. Use three of them in sentences of your own.

Harcourt

8 Journeys of Wonder

▲ **Practice Book, page 8**

Informative Writing

PARAGRAPH THAT COMPARES

Connect Writing to Reading

Remind students that in "Coyote Places the Stars," Coyote created the ladder to the moon and then used his bow and arrows to shape the stars. Ask students to name some of the ways in which Coyote's star pictures are alike. (Possible responses: Each has the form of one of Coyote's animal friends; they were all created for the same reason—so people would remember Coyote and the other animals of the canyon.) Explain that learning to write comparisons will help students recognize and make comparisons when they read.

Teach/Model

Display Transparency 3 and discuss it with students. Emphasize that paying attention to the points you are going to talk about will help them write clear and effective comparisons.

STUDENT MODEL:
PARAGRAPH THAT COMPARES

In a paragraph that compares, a writer shows how people, places, or things are alike. Here is a paragraph that compares two star groups. It was written by a student for science class.

topic sentence	*The Big Dipper and the Little Dipper are alike in several ways.*
examples of likeness	*First, both star groups look like dippers, long-handled cups used to dip water out of a bucket. Second, each star group also looks like a bear. Third, both star groups have seven bright stars that you can see right away. Four of the stars in each group form the bear's body, and the other three form its long tail.*
main point restated/ conclusion drawn	*It's amazing that these two star groups are so much alike.*

▲ Teaching Transparency 3

ANALYZE THE MODEL

- Audience—a teacher
- Writer's task—to show how two star groups are alike
- Examples of likenesses writer gives—both look like water dippers; both also look like bears; both have seven bright stars

FOCUS ON ORGANIZATION

- First sentence tells what's being compared.
- Likenesses appear in a logical order.
- Last sentence summarizes and draws a conclusion.

FOCUS ON ELABORATION

- Details explain several likenesses. (*dippers, long-handled cups used to dip water out of a bucket;* four stars for the body, three for the tail)
- Specific, vivid words (*long-handled cups, dip water out of a bucket, seven bright stars*) are used to describe likenesses and create interest.

Writing Prompts

Choose one of the following:

A Assign a prompt, for example:
Write a paragraph for classmates that compares two animals you know about. Give examples of ways the animals are alike. Be sure your examples are in a logical order.

B Have students write a paragraph that compares two persons, places, or things of their own choosing.

TECHNOLOGY

Students can use a word processing program such as *ClarisWorks for Kids*® to plan and write their paragraphs that compare.

Prewrite and Draft

Have students choose what they will compare and decide what main point they want to make. Students may use a graphic organizer like that on Transparency 4, to record their main ideas and organize their examples.

PARAGRAPH THAT COMPARES

Topic:	Audience:
Main Idea:	
Likeness 1: Details: Likeness 2: Details: Likeness 3: Details:	
Main Point Summarized:	

▲ Teaching Transparency 4

Revise

Have students work in pairs or small groups to discuss their paragraphs that compare. To help students work together constructively, provide the following questions:

- **Does the first sentence clearly state what is being compared?**
- **Do you give at least three likenesses that support your topic sentence?**
- **Do your sentences include details that explain the likenesses for your audience?**
- **Are your likenesses in a logical order?**
- **Does the last sentence summarize the comparison or draw a conclusion about it?**

After students have discussed each other's writing, have them revise their own paragraphs that compare.

SCORING RUBRIC FOR SUGGESTED PROMPT

4 Advanced The topic sentence clearly states what is being compared. The writer provides at least three likenesses that support the main idea and are presented in a meaningful order. Details add information about each likeness. The writer ends the paragraph with a summary or conclusion. The language is appropriate for the audience of classmates.

3 Proficient A topic sentence at the beginning states what is being compared. The writer offers at least three likenesses to support the main idea, and they are fairly well organized. However, the writer offers few details to explain the likenesses. The writer ends the paragraph by restating the main idea. The language is appropriate for the audience.

2 Basic A topic sentence states the main idea. Only one or two examples of likenesses support the comparison, and the writer offers few, if any, details. The last sentence restates the main idea. The writer does not use language that would interest the audience.

1 Below Basic The writer has not clearly stated a main idea in a topic sentence. The examples do not support the idea well, and the paragraph contains few details. The examples are not presented in a meaningful order. The writer forgets the audience and does not use language that makes the likenesses clear.

Assessment

STUDENT SELF- AND PEER-ASSESSMENT
Give students copies of the four-point scoring rubric, page R82, and have them suggest other important points. They may use the rubric to evaluate their own and/or each other's paragraphs that compare.

PORTFOLIO OPPORTUNITY
Students may keep their revised pieces in their work portfolios and complete their pieces later.

Test Prep

Remind students that during writing tests they should
- make sure they understand the prompt.
- begin with a topic sentence that states what is being compared.
- provide details about each likeness.

INFORMATIVE WRITING—EXPLANATION

Additional lessons:
Paragraph That Contrasts T96
Paragraph That Classifies T136
Complete Writing Process: T180
Tested or Timed Writing: T226

Language Handbook, pages 48–49, 53

GRAMMAR

Adjectives

SKILL TRACE	
INTRODUCE	T46–T47
Review	T69

Language Handbook, pages 116–117

REACHING ALL LEARNERS

ESL

Have students use adjective/noun pairs, such as *smart Coyote*, to practice forming sentences with adjectives after the verb: *Coyote was smart*. Begin with the following pairs:

still night

bright star

DAY 1 Teach/Model

DAILY LANGUAGE PRACTICE

1. **Some starrs in the sky look like a drawing of a bare.** (stars; bear)
2. **how did these shaps come to be** (How; shapes; be?)

INTRODUCE THE CONCEPT Display sentences 1–5 on Transparency 5 as you discuss these points:

- An **adjective** is a word that describes a noun.
- An adjective can come before the noun it describes.
- An adjective can follow a verb such as *is* or *seems*.

Have a volunteer find the adjective that describes *idea* in sentence 4. (*clever*) Point out that sentence 5 says the same thing in a different way.

Challenge students to complete sentence 6 using three different adjectives.

ADJECTIVES

1. **Coyote used a bow and arrow.**
2. **Skillful Coyote used a bow and arrow.**
3. **Coyote was skillful with a bow and arrow.**
4. **Coyote had a clever idea.** (*clever*)
5. **Coyote's idea was clever.**
6. **The ________ arrow whistled through the air.**

▲ Teaching Transparency 5

DAY 2 Extend the Concept

DAILY LANGUAGE PRACTICE

1. **Coyote moved the stars by shooting arrows at they.** (them)
2. **Coyotes star fourms looked like animales.** (Coyote's; forms; animals)

BUILD ORAL LANGUAGE Pick an object in the classroom, and have students supply sentences that describe it. Begin with a sentence such as "The bookcase is full." Students might add "The bookcase is wooden," "The bookcase is white," and so on. Continue with other objects.

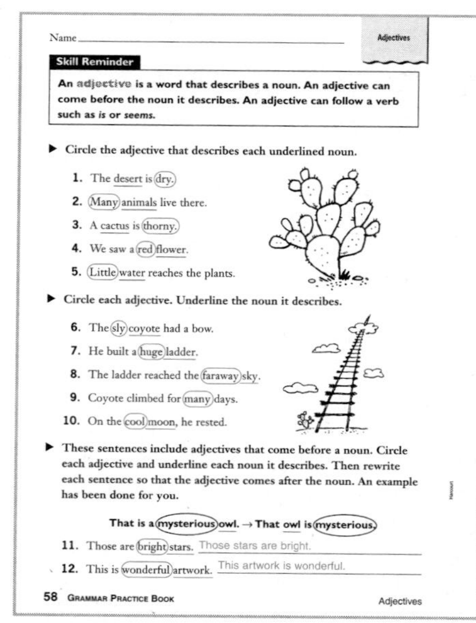

Name ______________________ Adjectives

Skill Reminder

An adjective is a word that describes a noun. An adjective can come before the noun it describes. An adjective can follow a verb such as *is* or *seems*.

▶ **Circle the adjective that describes each underlined noun.**

1. The desert is dry.
2. Many animals live there.
3. A cactus is thorny.
4. We saw a red flower.
5. Little water reaches the plants.

▶ **Circle each adjective. Underline the noun it describes.**

6. The sly coyote had a bow.
7. He built a huge ladder.
8. The ladder reached the faraway sky.
9. Coyote climbed for many days.
10. On the cool moon, he rested.

▶ **These sentences include adjectives that come before a noun. Circle each adjective and underline each noun it describes. Then rewrite each sentence so that the adjective comes after the noun. An example has been done for you.**

That is a mysterious owl. → That owl is mysterious.

11. Those are bright stars. Those stars are bright.
12. This is wonderful artwork. This artwork is wonderful.

Harcourt

58 GRAMMAR PRACTICE BOOK Adjectives

▲ **Grammar Practice Book, page 58**

DAY 3 Oral Review/Practice

DAILY LANGUAGE PRACTICE

1. **Us sat on the poarch and watched the rain.** (We; porch)
2. **during stoormes you cannot see the sky.** (During storms)

THE SKY IS DARK Write these sentences on the board:

It is a dark sky.

The sky is dark.

Have a volunteer identify each adjective and the noun it describes. *(dark, sky)* Then ask other students to come to the board and write pairs of sentences that are structured similarly. Have volunteers find the adjective and noun in each sentence.

Name ____________ Adjectives

▶ **Read the story about Coyote. Circle ten adjectives. Underline the nouns they describe.**

1.–10. Coyote woke on a (cold) <u>morning</u>. He met (big) <u>Bear</u> and (tiny) <u>Roadrunner</u> near the river.

"We are going to race," said Bear. "Who will win? Make a guess."

Coyote thought for a (long) <u>minute</u>. <u>Bear</u> was (strong.) <u>Roadrunner</u> was (fast.) "I choose Roadrunner," he said.

Away they ran. Suddenly Bear stepped on a (sharp) <u>stone</u>. Then Roadrunner tripped over a (spiny) <u>cactus</u>. The <u>runners</u> were (sad.)

"Cheer up," said Coyote. "Both of you win, and you can still be (best) <u>friends</u>."

▶ **Use each adjective in the box to write a sentence about Coyote.**
11.–14. Sentences will vary.

clever	happy	noisy	proud

11. ____________
12. ____________
13. ____________
14. ____________

Adjectives — Grammar Practice Book 59

▲ **Grammar Practice Book, page 59**

DAY 4 Apply to Writing

DAILY LANGUAGE PRACTICE

1. **how bright the full moon is?** (How; is!)
2. **i can see only foar large stars.** (I; four)

LISTS OF ADJECTIVES Have students work in pairs to write all the adjectives they can think of that describe the nouns *star* and *moon*. When students' lists are complete, they should write two sentences for each noun using their adjectives.

Test Prep

Remind students of these facts about adjectives:

- An adjective gives more information about a noun.
- Adjectives can come before the word they describe, or they may follow a verb such as *is*, *are*, *was*, *were*, or *seems*.

Name ____________ Coyote Places the Stars — Grammar: Adjectives

▶ **Circle the adjective in each sentence. Underline the noun it describes.**

1. (Graceful) <u>deer</u> moved across the desert.
2. The <u>lizards</u> were (slow.)
3. (Silvery) <u>fish</u> splashed up the stream.
4. A (great) <u>eagle</u> soared in the sky.
5. <u>Coyote</u> was (glad.)

▶ **Think of an adjective to describe each underlined noun. Rewrite the sentence, adding the adjective.**
Possible adjectives are given.

6. Coyote was an <u>artist</u>. — famous
7. He made a <u>ladder</u> to the moon. — tall
8. He moved the stars with <u>arrows</u>. — special
9. Now the stars make <u>pictures</u>. — beautiful
10. The pictures light the <u>sky</u>. — nighttime

TRY THIS! Think of a scene you might see from your window at night. Write five sentences to describe it. Circle the adjectives you used.

Journeys of Wonder 9

▲ **Practice Book, page 9**

DAY 5 Cumulative Review

DAILY LANGUAGE PRACTICE

1. **you and me will sing a song.** (You and I)
2. **Do you sing in the choorus.** (chorus?)

PRONOUNS AND ADJECTIVES Have students copy the following sentences and draw one line under each subject pronoun and two lines under each object pronoun. Then have them circle each adjective.

1. <u>He</u> relaxed in the (cool) grass.
2. The stars seemed (far) from <u>him</u>.
3. The (bright) moon pleased <u>them</u>.

Name ____________ Cumulative Review

▶ **Underline the correct pronoun of the two in parentheses ( ).**

1. **(<u>We</u>, Us)** like the view of the desert.
2. The hotel manager is speaking to **(I, <u>me</u>)**.
3. **(<u>She</u>, Her)** warns us about the coyotes.
4. Please describe them to **(we, <u>us</u>)**.
5. **(<u>I</u>, Me)** heard a coyote last night.

▶ **Think of an adjective to describe each underlined noun. Rewrite the sentence, adding the adjective.**
6.–10. Adjectives used in rewritten sentences will vary.

6. I admire the <u>cactus</u>.
7. What a <u>view</u> this is!
8. A <u>lizard</u> basks in the sun.
9. Our <u>car</u> is parked outside.
10. The <u>sign</u> blinks off and on.

60 Grammar Practice Book — Subject and Object Pronouns, Adjectives

▲ **Grammar Practice Book, page 60**

SPELLING

Words with /ôr/

SPELLING WORDS

1. form*
2. fourth
3. war
4. storm
5. horse*
6. warn
7. morning
8. forest
9. court
10. porch

BONUS WORDS

11. important
12. forward

*Words appearing in "Coyote Places the Stars." Additional story words following the generalization are *porcupines, formed,* and *chorus.*

STUDENT-CHOSEN WORDS

13. __________
14. __________
15. __________

REACHING ALL LEARNERS — CHALLENGE

Challenge more-proficient spellers by having them add the Bonus Words to their weekly spelling list. Include the words in their pretest and posttest, and encourage students to use them in the Spelling Activities.

DAY 1 Pretest/Self-Check

ADMINISTER THE PRETEST. Say each word, and then use it in a Dictation Sentence. Help students self-check their pretests using the list at the top of Transparency 6.

OPEN SORT Have students look for ways to sort the Spelling Words. For example, they might sort them according to the number of syllables or put them in alphabetical order. Ask volunteers to share their categories and sorted lists.

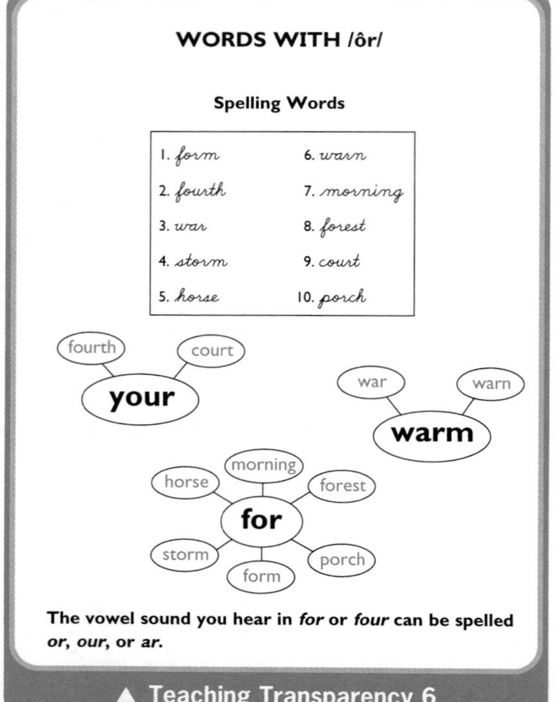

WORDS WITH /ôr/

Spelling Words

1. form	6. warn
2. fourth	7. morning
3. war	8. forest
4. storm	9. court
5. horse	10. porch

The vowel sound you hear in *for* or *four* can be spelled *or, our,* or *ar.*

▲ Teaching Transparency 6

DAY 2 Teach/Model

CLOSED SORT Display Transparency 6, or write the information on the board. Ask students to copy the webs and to write each Spelling Word where it belongs.

Have students use the words *form* and *storm* in sentences. Ask what the vowel sound is in both words. (the /ôr/ sound) Have a volunteer circle the letters that stand for this sound. Repeat the procedure with *fourth* and *war.* Ask students to identify how the /ôr/ sound is spelled in these words. (*our* and *ar*)

Handwriting Tip

Remind students to space letters properly so that they are easy to read. To illustrate this, write the word *horse* on the board.

horse

Name __________ Coyote Places the Stars Words with /ôr/

▶ Write the Spelling Word from the box that best completes each sentence.

storm horse morning forest

I like to ride my (1) horse. One (2) morning we left at dawn. We rode into the (3) forest. When it looked as if a (4) storm was coming, we went back home.

▶ Write the Spelling Word that fits each shape.

fourth war warn court

5. f o u r t h 7. w a r
6. c o u r t 8. w a r n

Handwriting Tip: When you join *o* to another letter, be sure that it doesn't look like an *a*. Write these words.

or

9. form ______ 10. porch ______

10 Journeys of Wonder

▲ Practice Book, page 10

DAY 3 Spelling Strategies

COMPARING SPELLINGS Write the following words on the board:

horse court warn

Have students read the words. Ask: What vowel sound do you hear in each word? What letters stand for that vowel sound? Suggest that when more than one combination of letters can spell the same vowel sound, students might want to write the word with all its possible spellings and compare them to see which looks right.

Apply to Writing

Have students use the strategy of comparing spellings as they proofread their writing. Have them look for words with the /ôr/ sound to be sure they have spelled the words correctly.

Name ________

SPELLING WORDS

1. form
2. fourth
3. war
4. storm
5. horse
6. warn
7. morning
8. forest
9. court
10. porch

SPELLING STRATEGY

Comparing Spellings

When you proofread and find a word that looks misspelled, try writing it another way. Compare the two spellings. Check which spelling is correct.

Words like *form, warn,* and *fourth*

▶ **Decide which of the two spellings for each pair looks correct. Check it with your Spelling Words. Then write the correctly spelled word.**

1. form *or* fourm? form
2. war *or* wor? war
3. wourn *or* warn? warn
4. forest *or* fourest? forest

▶ **Read the letter. Look at the two spellings in parentheses for each Spelling Word. Circle the correct spelling, and then write it.**

Dear Mom and Dad,

I am having fun at Uncle Jack's farm. Every **(5)** **(morning, marning)** I feed the chickens. The **(6)** **(farth, fourth)** day I was here, I helped milk the cows. I rode a big **(7)** **(harse, horse)** all by myself. We play tennis on the tennis **(8)** **(court, cort)**. One day I watched a **(9)** **(storm, starm)** from the **(10)** **(pourch, porch)**.

Love,
Sam

5. morning
6. fourth
7. horse
8. court
9. storm
10. porch

46 SPELLING PRACTICE BOOK LESSON 19

▲ Spelling Practice Book, page 46

DAY 4 Spelling Activities

SPELLING PASSWORD Write the Spelling Words from this lesson and some from a few previous lessons on pieces of paper—about twenty words in all. Divide the students into teams. Give a card to one player on each team. That player defines the word for teammates without using the word itself. If a teammate guesses the word and spells it correctly, the team gets a point. If not, the card is given back to you to be tried again later.

PICTURE DICTIONARY Tell students to divide three sheets of paper into four equal boxes. On a separate piece of paper, have them alphabetize their Spelling (and Bonus) Words. Then have them write one Spelling Word in each box, write their own definition of the word, and draw a picture of it.

Name ________

▶ **Word Find** Find seven Spelling Words and circle them. Then write them. Hint: Look for the letters *or, our,* and *ar.* Responses may be given in any order.

l	m	t	f	o	r	m
b	l	c	o	i	g	o
a	p	o	r	c	h	r
u	l	u	e	p	g	n
w	a	r	s	m	t	i
t	u	t	t	e	r	n
f	o	u	r	t	h	g

1. form
2. porch
3. war
4. fourth
5. court
6. forest
7. morning

▶ **A Cartoon** Finish the cartoon by circling the correct Spelling Words. Then write the Spelling Words.

"I **(8)** **(warn, wourn)** you! The sky is going to fall!" said the rooster.

"No, it's not. It's just a **(9)** **(sturm, storm)**!" said the **(10)** **(horse, hourse)**.

8. warn 9. storm 10. horse

▶ **What Am I?** Write the Spelling Word that answers each riddle.

11. I have four legs and run swiftly. horse
12. I am many trees close together. forest

SPELLING WORDS

1. form
2. fourth
3. war
4. storm
5. horse
6. warn
7. morning
8. forest
9. court
10. porch

LESSON 19 SPELLING PRACTICE BOOK 47

▲ Spelling Practice Book, page 47

DAY 5 Posttest

Assess students' progress using the Dictation Sentences.

DICTATION SENTENCES

1. **form** Some of the stars in the sky seem to form a bear.
2. **fourth** I sat in the fourth row of the classroom.
3. **war** We read about the war for independence.
4. **storm** The storm last night blew down many tree branches.
5. **horse** Doug feeds his horse carrots for a treat.
6. **warn** The weather report will warn us if a storm is coming.
7. **morning** Mom gets up early each morning to jog.
8. **forest** There are hiking trails in the forest near our house.
9. **court** At practice we had to run up and down the court.
10. **porch** We like to eat dinner on our back porch during the summer.

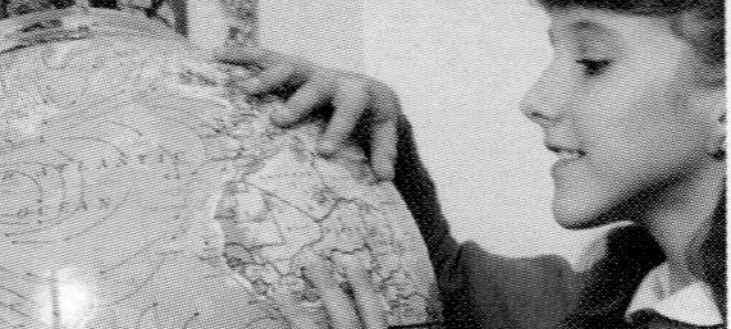

Cross-Curricular Connections

MULTI-AGE CLASSROOMS

If it is possible to access the public library's electronic card catalog via a classroom computer, have experienced students show others how to navigate and use the catalog.

INTERVENTION

Schedule a tour with a youth services librarian at the school or local library. Arrange for hands-on instruction or supervised practice in using the library's online catalog to locate books and other sources.

SCIENCE

Searching for the Great Bear

MATERIALS

- paper
- pencils

RESEARCH CONSTELLATIONS One version of how Ursa Major and other constellations came to be is told in "Coyote Places the Stars." Have students find and use astronomy references to find constellations that look like the ones described in the selection.

Independently or with partners, students should research a constellation and report back to the class, giving a few facts about stars in that constellation and telling the story behind its name.

Activity Card 32, page R13, will provide guidance for students doing library research. SPEAKING/READING/VIEWING

▶ Searching for the Great Bear ACTIVITY CARD 32

"Coyote Places the Stars" is a Native American tale of how the constellations came to be. Find a star map, and use it to find a constellation like those described in the story. Report what you learn to the class. In your report, give the names of some of the stars in the constellation. Also tell the story behind the constellation's name.

These steps will help you find star maps and other information:

- Do a subject search in the library's electronic card catalog. (Type in the word *constellations* and see what book titles come up on the screen.)
- Look for books with *J* in front of their call numbers to identify books in the young people's, or *juvenile*, collection.
- Use the books' tables of contents to look for the information you need.

▲ Activity Card 32

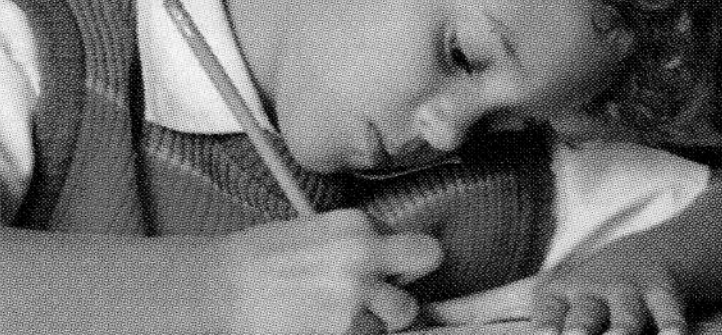

ART

The Batik Technique

MATERIALS
- a computer with Internet access
- drawing paper
- wax crayons
- thick brushes
- watercolors

FOLLOW DIRECTIONS Harriet Peck Taylor's batiks are unusual book illustrations. Have students look in art books and use the Internet to view more examples of batik works.

Encourage students to create batik-like pictures. Read aloud these directions, and then read them again one step at a time as students carefully follow along:

- Use a light-colored crayon to draw a simple picture on white paper.
- Add details to your picture.
- Brush dark watercolor over your paper.

Remind students that if they have questions they should wait until you pause, raise their hands, and ask politely.

FOCUS SKILL After students follow the instructions, have them discuss why it was necessary for them to pay close attention to sequence. READING REFERENCE SOURCES/VIEWING/REPRESENTING

RESEARCH

Inquiry Projects

"Coyote Places the Stars" can launch student inquiries into a variety of topics and ideas. Have students brainstorm topics they would like to know more about, and write them in a web. Some of the resources shown here can help them begin their own inquiry projects.

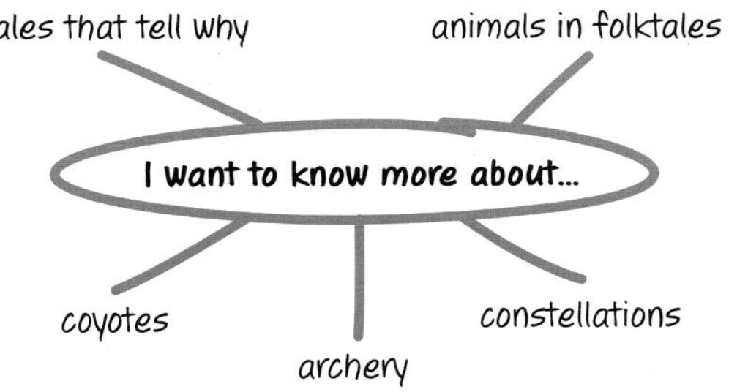

RESOURCES

Coyote Steals the Blanket by Janet Stevens. Holiday House, 1993. EASY

The Big Dipper by Franklyn M. Branley. HarperCollins, 1991. EASY

Stargazers by Gail Gibbons. Holiday House, 1992. AVERAGE

Why the Sky Is Far Away by Mary-Joan Gerson. Little, Brown, 1995. CHALLENGING

LESSON PREVIEW

"Why Mosquitoes Buzz in

THEME

Tell Me a Story

GENRE

Folktale

- **Retells** a story that was first told orally and passed down.
- Purpose is **to entertain** but may also teach a lesson.
- Shares the **beliefs** and **customs** of a culture.

CROSS-CURRICULAR CONNECTIONS

- **SCIENCE:** Exploring the Serengeti
- **MUSIC:** Sounds of the Forest

FOCUS STRATEGY USE TEXT STRUCTURE AND FORMAT

- **Before Reading:** Strategy Reminder on page T61
- **During Reading:** Apply the Strategy on pages T70, T74, T76

FOCUS SKILL SYLLABICATION

- **Before Reading:** Introduce the Skill on pages T60–T61
- **During Reading:** Apply the Skill on pages T66, T74
- **After Reading:** Practice the Skill on pages T92–T93

COMPANION SELECTION

- **"The Ant and the Dove"**
  Genre: Fable

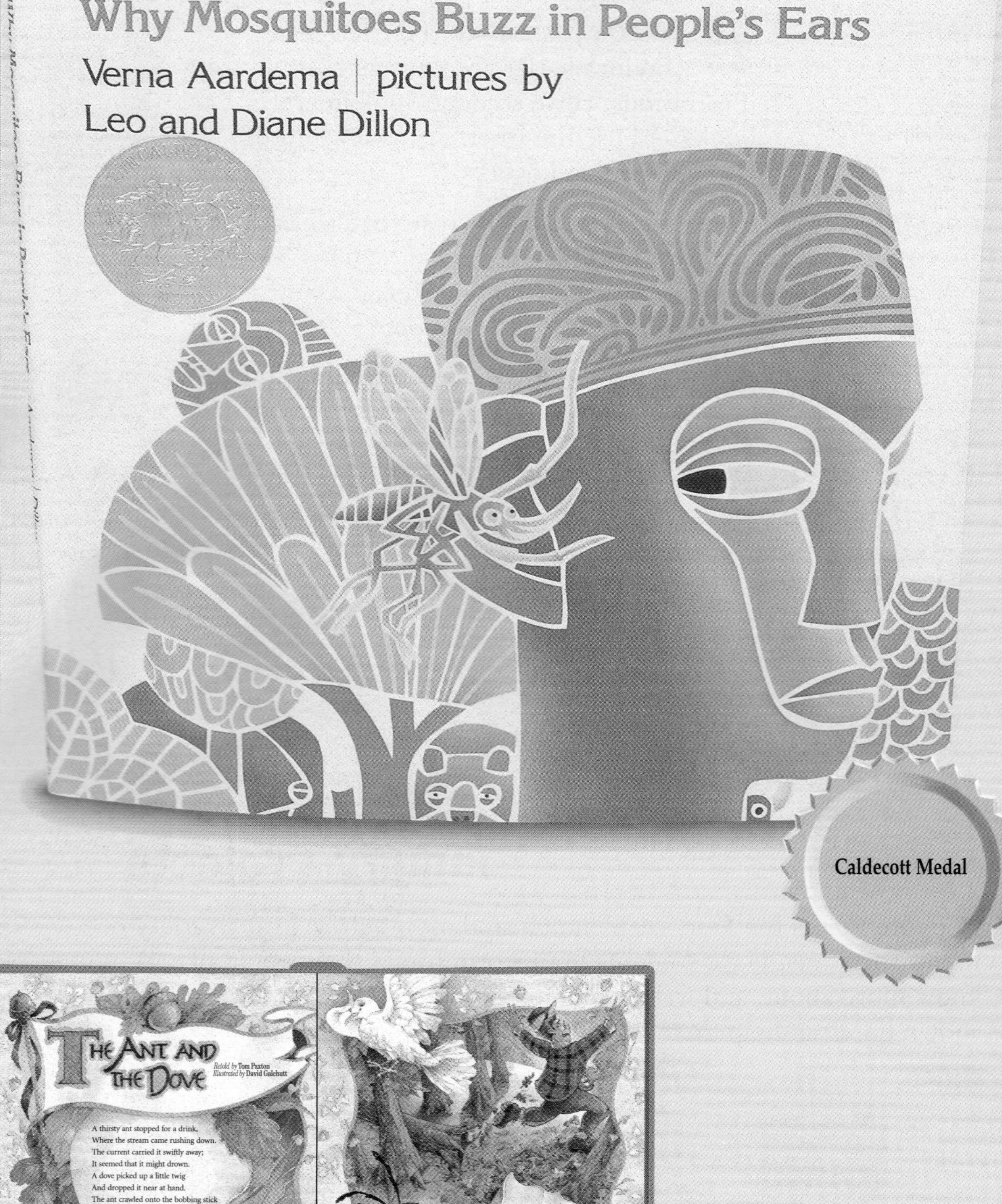

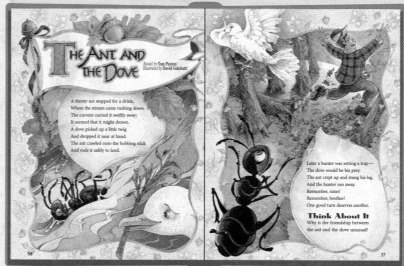

▲ **Student Edition, pages 56–57**

"Why Mosquitoes Buzz in People's Ears" illustrates pourquoi tales that are passed down from generation to generation to answer questions about the world.

Selection Summary

The iguana puts sticks in his ears so he doesn't have to listen to a silly story the mosquito tells him. Because of the sticks, the iguana doesn't hear the python's greeting. Thus begins a chain of events and misunderstandings that results in the death of a baby owl. When Mother Owl will not wake the sun so day can come, King Lion calls a council meeting. The facts about the owlet's death are slowly revealed and so is the answer to the question, "Why do mosquitoes buzz in people's ears?"

Author Profile

Verna Aardema began writing stories to make her daughter eat her dinner. Aardema told her daughter stories about Africa because she read a lot about it. Since the days of her "feeding" stories, Aardema has written many books and won numerous awards.

Illustrator Profile

Shortly after **Leo** and **Diane Dillon** met at the Parsons School of Design in New York, they married. After collaborating on a variety of projects, they found success as illustrators of children's books. The Dillons received the 1976 Caldecott Medal for "Why Mosquitoes Buzz in People's Ears."

REACHING ALL LEARNERS

BELOW-LEVEL READERS

EASY READER
"Grandpa Tells Why," pp. 134–141. Reinforces selection vocabulary and these additional words from "Why Mosquitoes Buzz in People's Ears":

terrified danger meeting

See *New Adventures Intervention Reader Teacher's Guide,* pp. 98–103.

CASSETTE
"Why Mosquitoes Buzz in People's Ears" is available on *Literature Cassette 3.*

CHALLENGE

Fire on the Mountain by Jane Kurtz. Aladdin, 1998. CHALLENGING

INQUIRY PROJECTS
See page T103. Students can brainstorm topics related to "Why Mosquitoes Buzz in People's Ears." Encourage them to raise questions and then plan and carry out research.

SUGGESTED

LESSON PLANNER

WHY MOSQUITOES BUZZ IN PEOPLE'S EARS

Skills and Strategies	PRETEACHING AND READING — DAY 1	READING AND RESPONDING — DAY 2
Reading Listening Speaking Viewing **Vocabulary** nonsense grumbling mischief duty council summons satisfied	**BUILDING BACKGROUND AND CONCEPTS** T58 **INTRODUCING VOCABULARY** T59 *Transparency 7* *Practice Book* p. 11 **PRETEACHING SKILLS** Before Reading FOCUS SKILL Syllabication (Introduce) T60–T61 *Transparency 8* FOCUS STRATEGY Use Text Structure and Format T61 **PREREADING STRATEGIES** T62 **READING THE SELECTION** T62–T85  *Literature Cassette 3* Illustrator Information T85 **ALTERNATIVE SELECTION** Easy Reader: "Grandpa Tells Why" **NOTE: Students may begin reading the selection on Day 2.**	**LITERARY RESPONSE** T82 Return to the Predictions/Purpose Appreciating the Literature **THINK ABOUT IT** T82 **RETELL AND SUMMARIZE** T83 *Practice Book* p. 13 **STUDY AND RESEARCH SKILLS** ✔ Locating Information (Maintain) T67 **REREADING FOR FLUENCY** Readers Theatre T90 **LITERATURE RESPONSE** A Summons T90 *Activity Card 33*, R14 **INTERVENTION STRATEGIES FOR BELOW-LEVEL READERS** T91 FOCUS STRATEGY Rereading Language Exploration
Writing	**Informative Writing: Paragraph That Contrasts** Connect Writing to Reading T96	Teach/Model T96 Analyze the Model *Transparency 10* *Language Handbook* p. 54
Grammar	**Adjectives for *What Kind*** Teach/Model T98 *Transparency 12* *Language Handbook* pp. 120–121	Extend the Concept T98 *Grammar Practice Book* p. 61
Daily Language Practice	**1. Suppose the sun did not rise one day?** (day.) **2. i could never imagine such a thinge.** (I, thing)	**1. Oure class read a story. About the sunn.** (Our; story about; sun) **2. the story comes from africa.** (The; Africa)
Spelling	**Homophones** one won hour way heard flower our flour weigh herd Pretest/Self-Check T100 *Transparency 13*	Teach/Model T100 *Practice Book* p. 17 Handwriting Tip

KEY

✔ **Tested Skills**

■ **Management Option:** See Managing the Classroom, page T56, for ongoing independent activities.

Reaching All Learners: Support for "Grandpa Tells Why," an alternative selection, appears on *Intervention Reader Teacher's Guide*, pp. 98–103.

READING AND RESPONDING

DAY 3

COMPANION SELECTION
"The Ant and the Dove" T86–T87

RESPONSE ACTIVITIES
Tell a Story T88
Create a Pourquoi Tale T88
■ Publishing Station
Write a Report T89
Write a Story T89

Selection Comprehension Test

GRAMMAR
Adjectives (Review) T69

ORAL LANGUAGE
A Debate T90
■ Listening Station

VIEWING
Cut-out Designs T90

INDEPENDENT READING
Reader's Choice Library:
The Wave T57

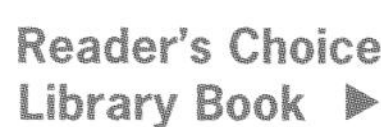
Reader's Choice Library Book ▶

Writing Prompts T96
Prewrite and Draft T97
Transparency 11
 *ClarisWorks for Kids®*

Oral Review/Practice T99
Grammar Practice Book p. 62

1. **Meny storys are about animals.** (Many stories)
2. **Sometimes our teacher reads stores to we.** (stories to us)

Spelling Strategies T101
Apply to Writing
Spelling Practice Book p. 48

EXTENDING SKILLS & STRATEGIES

DAY 4

COMPREHENSION
After Reading
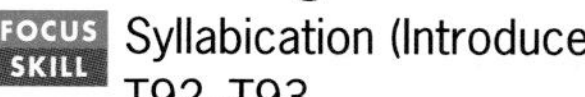
FOCUS SKILL Syllabication (Introduce) T92–T93
Transparency 9
Practice Book p. 14

DECODING/PHONICS
Vowel Variants: /o͞o/*ou, ough* (Maintain) T71

VOCABULARY T94–T95
Reviewing Vocabulary Words
Extending Vocabulary
Practice Book p. 15

TAKE-HOME BOOK
The World Next Door T94

CROSS-CURRICULAR CONNECTIONS
Science: Exploring the Serengeti T102
Activity Card 34, R14
FOCUS SKILL Apply Syllabication
Computer Station T56

Take-Home Book ▶

Revise T97

Apply to Writing T99
Practice Book p. 16

1. **in this story. A little mosquito makes a big mistake.** (In this story a)
2. **the owl must hoot each daye to wake the sun.** (The; day)

Spelling Activities T101
Spelling Practice Book p. 49

EXTENDING SKILLS & STRATEGIES

DAY 5

COMPREHENSION
✔ Sequence (Review) T75
Practice Book p. 12

CROSS-CURRICULAR CONNECTIONS
Music: Sounds of the Forest T103

INQUIRY PROJECTS T103
Research

SELF-SELECTED READING T57
- *How the Ostrich Got Its Long Neck*
- *Anansi and the Talking Melon*
- *Bugs and Other Insects*

Assessment T97
Student Self- and Peer-Assessment
Scoring Rubric

Cumulative Review T99
Grammar Practice Book p. 63

1. **The king calls a meeting. Because Mother Owl does not hoot?** (meeting because; does not hoot.)
2. **He lerns that Mother Owl is to sad to hoot.** (learns; too sad)

Posttest T101

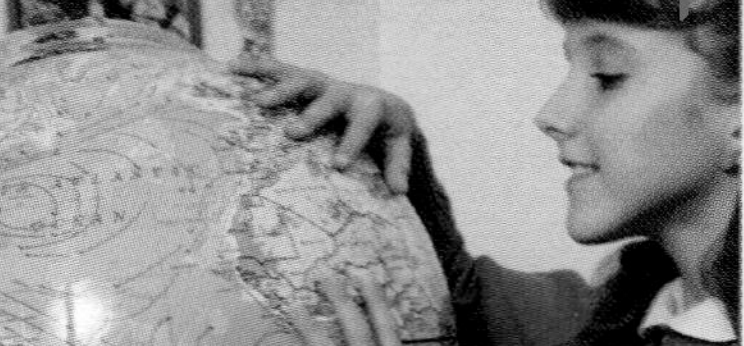

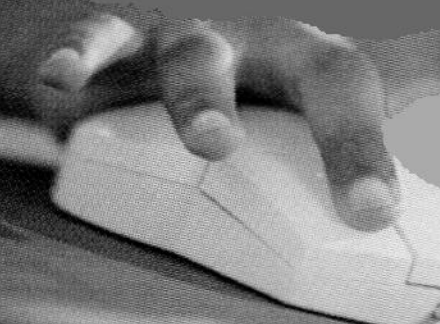

Managing the Classroom

While you provide direct instruction to individuals or small groups, other students can work on ongoing activities like the ones below.

Listening Station

OBJECTIVE
To record and listen for musical elements of language

MATERIALS
- tape recorder
- cassettes
- paper and markers

See page T90 for the Oral Language activity. Students can tape-record and listen to their choral reading presentations for enjoyment. As students listen, have them record on a chart the number of times they hear sounds repeated and instances of onomatopoeia.

Repeated Sounds	Onomatopoeia
卌 III	IIII

Art Station

OBJECTIVE
To draw a favorite character from the story

MATERIALS
- paper
- crayons, markers

Have students draw their favorite character from the story in as much detail as they can to show that character's personality. Encourage them to add scenery that recalls the story setting.

Publishing Station

OBJECTIVE
To write and publish a pourquoi tale

MATERIALS
- paper, markers
- pencils
- hole punch
- yarn or string

Have students write and illustrate their own pourquoi tales about why something is or acts a certain way. They can use a hole punch and bind the pages together with yarn. Remind students to proofread their writing for spelling errors.

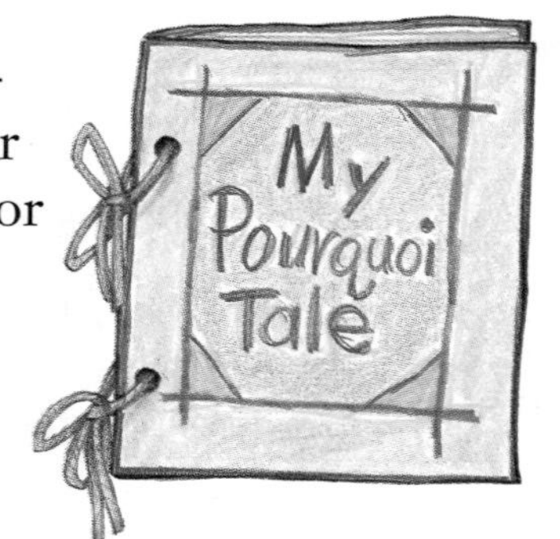

Computer Station

OBJECTIVE
To use a computer program to make a chart

MATERIALS
- computer with a word processing program and chart function

After students complete the activity on page T102, they can use a word processing program and clip art to make a chart of the multisyllable science-related words they encountered in their research.

Note: For more options, see pages T88–T89, T90–T91, and T102–T103.

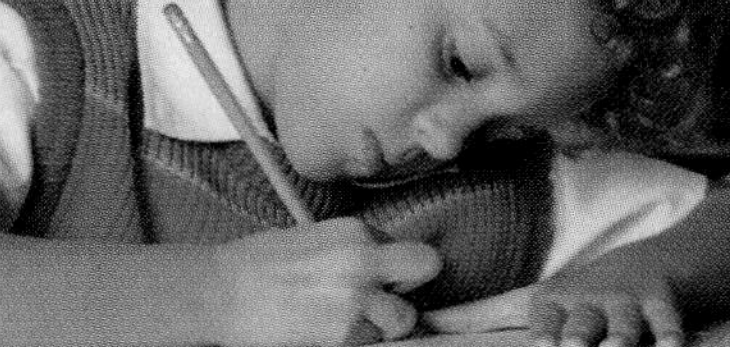

GUIDED READING

Multi-Level Books

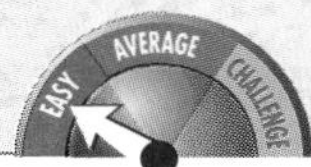

EASY

How the Ostrich Got Its Long Neck by Verna Aardema. Scholastic, 1995. FOLKTALE: SELECTION AUTHOR

EASY READER: NEW ADVENTURES
"Grandpa Tells Why," pp. 134–141

TAKE-HOME BOOK
The World Next Door NONFICTION: PERSONAL NARRATIVE/ SCIENCE

LEVELED LIBRARY BOOK
Coyote: A Trickster Tale from the American Southwest by Gerald McDermott. FOLKTALE: ORAL TRADITION

AVERAGE

Anansi Finds a Fool by Verna Aardema. Dial, 1992. FOLKTALE: SELECTION AUTHOR

Anansi and the Talking Melon by Eric A. Kimmel. Holiday House, 1995. FOLKTALE: AFRICA

READER'S CHOICE LIBRARY
The Wave by Margaret Hodges. FOLKTALE: TRADITIONAL TALE

See the **Reader's Choice Library lesson plan** on pages T236–T237.

CHALLENGING

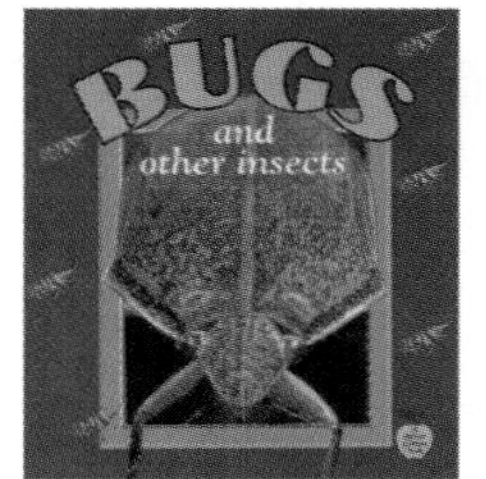

Bugs and Other Insects by Bobbie Kalman and Tammy Everts. Crabtree, 1994. NONFICTION: BUGS

Fire on the Mountain by Jane Kurtz. Aladdin, 1998. FOLKTALE: AFRICA

Bugs by Nancy Winslow Parker and Joan Richards Wright. William Morrow, 1987. NONFICTION: BUGS

Building Background and Concepts

ESL

See *ESL Manual* pages 98–103. You may wish to introduce these additional words:

yam (page 35)
plotting (page 37)
alarm (page 37)
fault (page 41)
startled (page 43)

OTHER BACKGROUND-BUILDING IDEAS

Read-Aloud Anthology, "The Clever Warthog," pages 57–58.

INTERNET Bonus words and additional background ideas can be found on *The Learning Site* at **www.harcourtschool.com**

Access Prior Knowledge

Discuss pourquoi tales. Help students recall what happened in the folktale "Coyote Places the Stars." Ask students to explain what question about nature that story answered. (Possible response: how the constellations were arranged in the sky) Point out that besides answering questions about events in nature, folktales often teach lessons.

Develop Concepts

Begin a web about folktales. Have students begin a web about folktales. Ask questions that lead students to add vocabulary to the web: **What kinds of lessons do folktales teach? Are the characters and events real or *nonsense*?** Highlight indicates vocabulary.

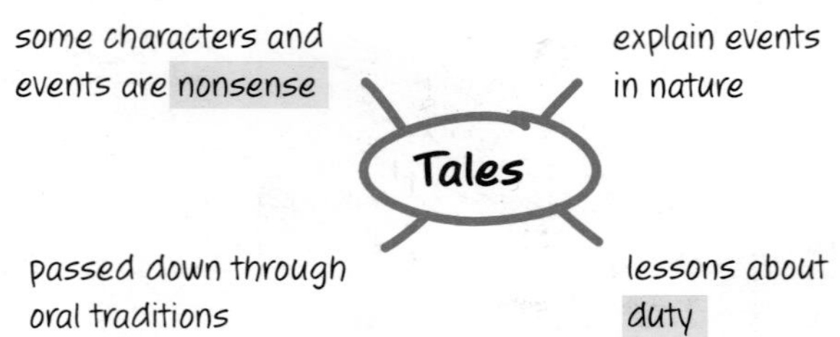

Then explain that "Why Mosquitoes Buzz in People's Ears" is a folktale that teaches a lesson about jumping to conclusions and that explains why mosquitoes always seem to buzz in people's ears.

BONUS WORDS

Introduce specialized vocabulary. If necessary, introduce the following animal words found in "Why Mosquitoes Buzz in People's Ears": *mosquito, iguana, python, antelope, owlet.*

Introducing Vocabulary

Build Word Identification Strategies

Use word order and context to confirm meaning.

Display Transparency 7, and have three volunteers read the skit aloud. Remind students that they can sometimes figure out new words by looking at the other words and sentences nearby. Model using word order and context to confirm the meaning of the word *grumbling*:

MODEL **As I read the first sentence, I can tell that *grumbling* is something worm is doing. In the next sentence I see the word *complain*. Grumbling must be one way to complain or show dissatisfaction.**

As students decode the other vocabulary, encourage them to confirm meanings and pronunciations through context, by asking **Are there other words nearby that help explain this word? Does it make sense? Should I use the glossary to check?**

CHECK UNDERSTANDING

Practice other vocabulary strategies. Have students place the vocabulary words in a predict-o-gram about the story. They should predict whether each word relates to the characters, the setting, or an event. Students can confirm their predictions in Reviewing Vocabulary Words, page T94. CLASSIFY/PREDICT

Predict-o-Gram		
Characters	Setting	Events
grumbling	council	nonsense

QUICKWRITE

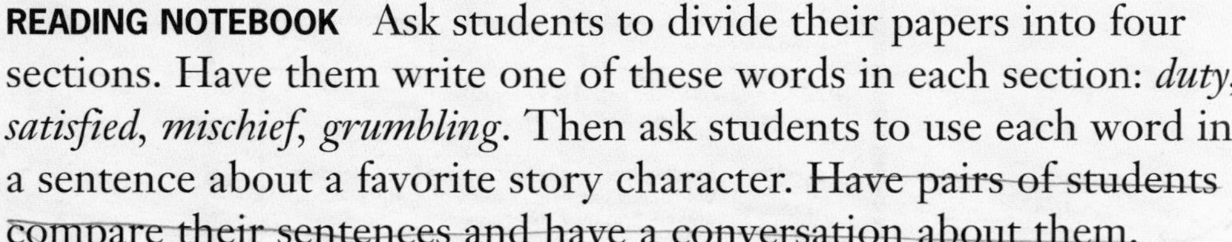

READING NOTEBOOK Ask students to divide their papers into four sections. Have them write one of these words in each section: *duty*, *satisfied*, *mischief*, *grumbling*. Then ask students to use each word in a sentence about a favorite story character. ~~Have pairs of students compare their sentences and have a conversation about them.~~

VOCABULARY DEFINED

nonsense words or ideas that are foolish and have no real meaning

grumbling complaining

mischief behavior that causes problems for others

duty a job; a responsibility

council a meeting called to find answers to questions

summons an important message to appear before a leader

satisfied have one's needs or desires fulfilled

VOCABULARY

CHARACTERS: Ant, Ladybug, and Worm

LADYBUG: (*sweetly*) What are you **grumbling** about now, Worm? Must you always complain?

WORM: (*in a low, gruff voice*) Some folks are never **satisfied.** I've done my **duty** as a member of the **council.** We solved every problem that came up this year. But is that enough? No!

ANT: (*whispers to Ladybug*) Worm got a **summons** to appear before Chief Garden Snake today.

WORM: This is that sneaky Beetle's fault. I just know it. He's always up to some **mischief.**

LADYBUG: That's **nonsense.** Beetle is your friend. Come on, I'll go to the meeting with you.

Ladybug, Ant, and Worm crawl to the garden. No one is around.

WORM: What's going on?

Garden creatures suddenly appear from under leaves and behind stems holding balloons and party favors.

EVERYONE: Surprise! Happy Birthday, Worm!

▲ Teaching Transparency 7

Name ______ Why Mosquitoes Buzz in People's Ears Vocabulary

▶ Complete each animal's sentence or sentences with a word from the box.

nonsense duty grumbling council mischief summons satisfied

1. I wonder what this __council__ meeting is all about.
2. I don't know. I just got the __summons__ this morning.
3. Maybe I've been __grumbling__ about the heat too much lately.
4. Maybe it's because I've been causing __mischief__ in the trees.
5. I feel it's my __duty__ to tell you that you've been staying up too late.
6. That's complete __nonsense__!
7. Quiet, everyone. Your curiosity is about to be __satisfied__.

▶ Answer the following questions with words from the box above.

8. If you cause a lot of trouble, what are you making? __mischief__
9. If you are responsible for doing a job, what do you have? a __duty__
10. If you are happy about someone or something, how do you feel? __satisfied__

TRY THIS! Imagine that animals can talk. Write a paragraph about a meeting of some pets. Use as many Vocabulary Words as you can.

Journeys of Wonder 11

▲ Practice Book, page 11

BEFORE READING

SKILL TRACE	
INTRODUCE	
• Before Reading:	T60–T61
• During Reading:	T66, T74
• After Reading:	T92–T93
Reteach	R3
Review	T273

OBJECTIVE:

To use syllabication to read unfamiliar words

Preview the Literature

Preview the selection and discuss the genre.

Invite students to look at the illustrations and tell where the story takes place. (in a forest or rain forest) Then have them silently read page 35.

Ask students: **How can you tell from the title of this story what it will be about? How is this folktale like "Coyote Places the Stars"?** Explain that this folktale comes from West Africa and that most cultures, or regions, pass down folktales that explain mysterious things.

Introduce the Skill

Discuss syllabication.

Explain to students that dividing a long word into syllables can help readers pronounce unfamiliar words. Display Transparency 8, or copy it on the board, and have a volunteer read the explanation of syllables and the tips for reading long words. Guide students through the examples.

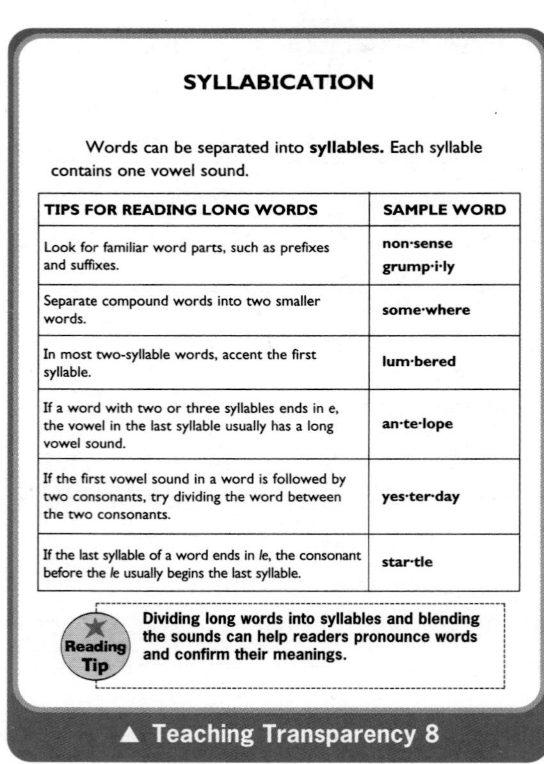

SYLLABICATION

Words can be separated into **syllables.** Each syllable contains one vowel sound.

TIPS FOR READING LONG WORDS	SAMPLE WORD
Look for familiar word parts, such as prefixes and suffixes.	**non·sense** **grump·i·ly**
Separate compound words into two smaller words.	**some·where**
In most two-syllable words, accent the first syllable.	**lum·bered**
If a word with two or three syllables ends in e, the vowel in the last syllable usually has a long vowel sound.	**an·te·lope**
If the first vowel sound in a word is followed by two consonants, try dividing the word between the two consonants.	**yes·ter·day**
If the last syllable of a word ends in *le*, the consonant before the *le* usually begins the last syllable.	**star·tle**

Reading Tip: **Dividing long words into syllables and blending the sounds can help readers pronounce words and confirm their meanings.**

▲ Teaching Transparency 8

Model the Thinking

Model using syllabication to pronounce unfamiliar words.

Read aloud and discuss with students the Reading Tip on Transparency 8. Then use the passage on *Student Edition* page 35 to model for students how to apply rules about syllables to pronounce the word *waterhole*.

MODEL **As I read page 35, I see a long word I don't know. I see that this is a compound word. I can separate it into two smaller words, *water* and *hole*. When I pronounce the smaller words together, the word sounds like *waterhole*. I guess it probably means "a hole with water in it."**

- Apply the Skill, pages T66, T74
- Practice the Skill, pages T92–T93

STRATEGY REMINDER

 FOCUS STRATEGY Use Text Structure and Format

Encourage students to monitor their comprehension.

Explain to students that in some stories certain words and phrases are repeated. Noticing when and how these repeated words and phrases are used can help them better understand the story and story characters. Invite volunteers to explain how the repetition of words and phrases might be helpful. (Possible responses: It can help readers predict what is coming next in the text. It can help readers understand how characters behave.)

- Apply the Strategy, pages T70, T74, T76

STRATEGIES GOOD READERS USE

- Use Prior Knowledge
- Make and Confirm Predictions
- Adjust Reading Rate
- Self-Question
- Create Mental Images
- Use Context to Confirm Meaning
- **Use Text Structure and Format** FOCUS STRATEGY
- Use Graphic Aids
- Use Reference Sources
- Read Ahead
- Reread
- Summarize

Prereading Strategies

PREVIEW AND PREDICT

Encourage students who have not yet previewed the selection to look at the illustrations and read page 35 to predict what this story might be about. Remind students that a folktale often has animal characters who behave like people. Have students begin a chart to keep track of the characters in "Why Mosquitoes Buzz in People's Ears." See *Practice Book* page 13.

Character Chart		
Character	What the Character Says	What the Character Does
mosquito	tells iguana a far-fetched story	annoys iguana

SET PURPOSE

Read to Be Entertained Have students set a purpose for reading "Why Mosquitoes Buzz in People's Ears." Remind them that thinking about their purpose for reading makes reading more meaningful. Ask students what their purpose for reading this tale is. (Possible response: to be entertained) If students have difficulty setting a purpose, offer this suggestion:

MODEL **As I previewed the story, I found out it has talking animal characters. I would like to find out what happens to these characters and why mosquitoes buzz in people's ears, according to this folktale.**

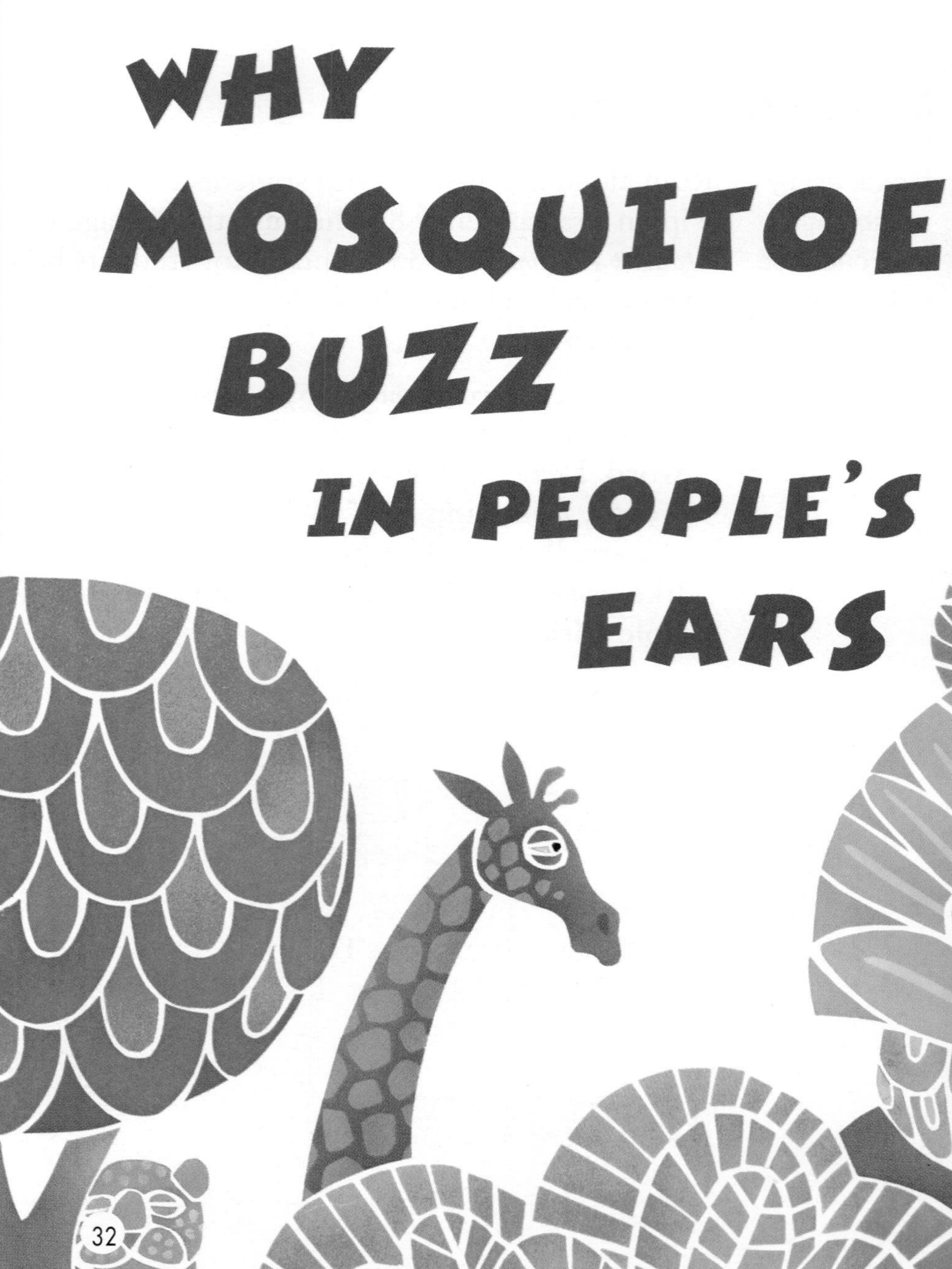

Options for Reading

DIRECTED READING The **Monitor Comprehension** questions offer a way to check students' comprehension. The **Guided Reading** strategies on pages T64, T66, T68, T70, T74 and T78 provide additional support.
WHOLE CLASS/SMALL GROUP

COOPERATIVE READING Have students reading on or above level use *Comprehension Card 5* (p. R10) to discuss **author's purpose.**
INDEPENDENT/SMALL GROUP

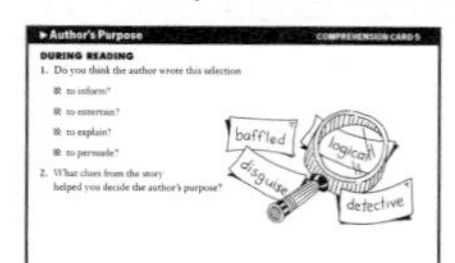

INDEPENDENT READING Encourage students to take notes about the strategies they use during reading. Suggest that they pause every few pages to discuss these strategies with a partner and explain how they help.
PAIRS/WHOLE CLASS

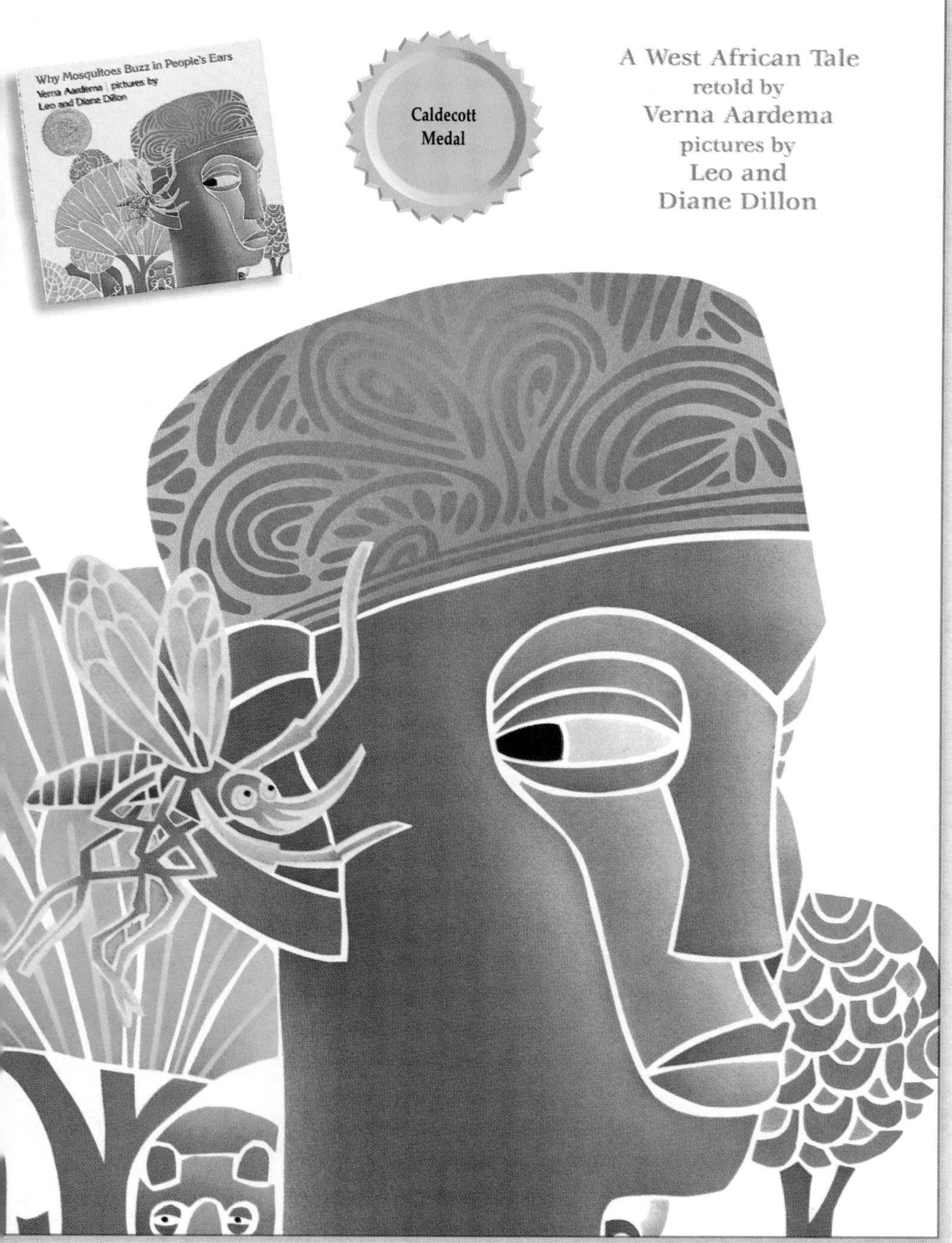

SKILLS IN CONTEXT

Informal Assessment

INTERVENTION STRATEGIES

MODIFIED INSTRUCTION Have students read the title, "Why Mosquitoes Buzz in People's Ears," and tell what they see on the first two pages. Discuss these story words:

listen sticks limb wake scared

Then have students read through page 39 and set a purpose for reading. (to find out what happens because of the sticks in Iguana's ears)

EASY READER Students may read "Grandpa Tells Why," found on pages 134–141 in ***New Adventures***. See ***New Adventures Intervention Reader Teacher's Guide*** pages 98–103.

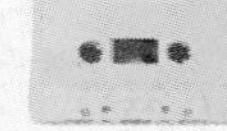

"Why Mosquitoes Buzz in People's Ears" and "The Ant and the Dove" are available on *Literature Cassette 3*.

Monitor Comprehension

1 **Why does the iguana put sticks in his ears?** (Mosquito tells him a foolish story about yams. Iguana puts the sticks in his ears so he won't have to listen to any more of mosquito's nonsense.) INFERENTIAL: CAUSE-EFFECT

2 **Why does the iguana say that mosquito's story about the yams is nonsense?** (Possible response: because a yam that was almost as big as a mosquito would be very, very tiny) INFERENTIAL: DRAW CONCLUSIONS

Guided Reading

STRATEGIES GOOD READERS USE

Create Mental Images If students have difficulty understanding why the iguana dismisses the mosquito's story about the yams as nonsense, work in a small group to discuss how creating mental images can help students check their understanding of what they read. Use these prompts:

- **Yams are similar to sweet potatoes. Picture an average-size sweet potato.**
- **Picture a mosquito.**
- **Now picture a sweet potato almost as big as the mosquito.**

AUTHOR'S CRAFT

MUSICAL ELEMENTS OF LANGUAGE The author has used sound words, such as *mek, mek* on page 35, to help readers imagine the animals as they move. Explain to students that the author repeats these words like the repetition of a song's refrain. Their use lends a musical quality to the text. Call on students to read the sound words in the story aloud, listening for their effect.

ONE MORNING a mosquito saw an iguana drinking at a waterhole. The mosquito said, "Iguana, you will never believe what I saw yesterday."

"Try me," said the iguana.

The mosquito said, "I saw a farmer digging yams that were almost as big as I am."

"What's a mosquito compared to a yam?" snapped the iguana grumpily. "I would rather be deaf than listen to such nonsense!" Then he stuck two sticks in his ears and went off, mek, mek, mek, mek, through the reeds.

35

REACHING ALL LEARNERS

ESL

SOUND WORDS Tell students that as they read they will come across many unusual words such as *mek, mek,* as well as words that stand for sounds the animals in the story make. Explain that these words are similar to more familiar words such as *quack quack* or *meow* that imitate the sounds animals make. Ask students to imitate animal sounds or the sounds of animal movements. (*swish swish* or *clip clop*)

Monitor Comprehension

1. **Why do you think the iguana does not answer the python?**
(Possible response: He doesn't hear him because he has sticks in his ears.)
INFERENTIAL: MAIN IDEA

2. **Read aloud the first sentence. What rule helped you pronounce the two-syllable words *grumbling* and *python* in this sentence?**
(Possible response: In most two-syllable words, the first syllable is accented.)
FOCUS SKILL METACOGNITIVE: SYLLABICATION

Guided Reading

STRATEGIES GOOD READERS USE

Reread If students have trouble understanding why the iguana doesn't answer the python, it may be because they have forgotten that the iguana put sticks in his ears. Have students reread page 35. You may wish to use this think-aloud:

MODEL **I know that the iguana did not answer the python but I'm not sure why. I remember that the iguana said he didn't want to listen to the mosquito's nonsense. I will go back and read that part again to see if it can help me.**

CULTURAL CONNECTIONS

COMPARE ORAL STORIES Read aloud a classic, repetitive poem such as "The House That Jack Built." Point out that traditional tales often use repetition and patterns. Have students share and compare oral stories they know from grandparents, parents, and other family members. Discuss the use of language in the stories and how they reflect different customs, regions, and cultures.

The iguana was still grumbling to himself when he happened to pass by a python.

The big snake raised his head and said, "Good morning, Iguana."

The iguana did not answer but lumbered on, bobbing his head, badamin, badamin.

"Now, why won't he speak to me?" said the python to himself. "Iguana must be angry about something. I'm afraid he is plotting some mischief against me!" He began looking for somewhere to hide. The first likely place he found was a rabbit hole, and in it he went, wasawusu, wasawusu, wasawusu.

When the rabbit saw the big snake coming into her burrow, she was terrified. She scurried out through her back way and bounded, krik, krik, krik, across a clearing.

A crow saw the rabbit running for her life. He flew into the forest crying kaa, kaa, kaa! It was his duty to spread the alarm in case of danger.

exception

37

SKILLS IN CONTEXT

STUDY AND RESEARCH SKILLS
TESTED SKILL

Locating Information

SKILL TRACE	
Introduce	T566, T592, 3-1
Reteach	R51, 3-1
Review 1	T617, 3-1
Review 2	T673, 3-1
Test	Theme 3, 3-1
Maintain	T67

TEACH/MODEL

Ask students to recall what they read on page 37 about where rabbits live. Then ask where they could find more information about rabbits. (encyclopedia, nature magazines, CD-ROMs, Internet sites)

Remind students that they can research topics at the library by looking in the card catalog or on a computer database. Both the card catalog and the database list books by title, by author, and by subject. Model using a card catalog or computer.

MODEL **To find information on rabbits, I look in the drawer with the letter R, or I type the word *rabbit* under *Subject.* I use the call number for each book listed for my topic to find the books on the library's shelves.**

PRACTICE/APPLY

Help students develop a list of topics related to the story. Ask them to explain where they would look and how they would locate information on each topic.

REACHING ALL LEARNERS

CHALLENGE

WARNING: DANGER Encourage small groups of students to discuss the crow's actions when he sees the rabbit running. Have them speculate on the kinds of danger forest animals would need to know about. Then ask them to keep these dangers in mind as they debate whether or not the crow should have spread the alarm. Invite students to share the results of their discussion with the class.

Monitor Comprehension

1 **What happened after the monkey heard the crow?** (Possible response: The monkey started screeching and leaping through the trees. When he jumped on a dead limb, the limb fell onto an owl nest and killed an owlet.)
INFERENTIAL: SUMMARIZE

2 **How do you know that Mother Owl has been deeply saddened by the death of her owlet?** (Possible response: The text says she was "so sad, so sad, so sad." She does not hoot for the sun so that dawn can come.)
METACOGNITIVE: INTERPRETING CHARACTER'S EMOTIONS

3 **What do you think the animals will do when they realize that Mother Owl is not going to wake the sun?** (Possible response: try to make her feel better; try to change her mind) INFERENTIAL: MAKE PREDICTIONS

Guided Reading

STRATEGIES GOOD READERS USE

Summarize If students have trouble telling what happened after the monkey heard the crow, work in a small group discussing how summarizing can help them check their comprehension. Ask these questions:

- **What did the monkey think when he heard the crow?**
- **How did he react?**

SCIENCE

EACH NEW DAY Remind students that in real life no creature is responsible for making the sun appear. If possible, use a three-dimensional model to illustrate that the earth is revolving, or spinning, as it orbits the sun. It takes 24 hours, or one day, for the earth to complete one rotation. The sun does not move, but as the earth rotates, the sun appears to rise and set.

A monkey heard the crow. He was sure that some dangerous beast was prowling near. He began screeching and leaping kili wili through the trees to help warn the other animals.

As the monkey was crashing through the treetops, he happened to land on a dead limb. It broke and fell on an owl's nest, killing one of the owlets.

baby animal

Mother Owl was not at home. For though she usually hunted only in the night, this morning she was still out searching for one more tidbit to satisfy her hungry babies. When she returned to the nest, she found one of them dead. Her other children told her that the monkey had killed it. All that day and all that night, she sat in her tree—so sad, so sad, so sad!

Now it was Mother Owl who woke the sun each day so that the dawn could come. But this time, when she should have hooted for the sun, she did not do it.

The night grew longer and longer. The animals of the forest knew it was lasting much too long. They feared that the sun would never come back.

39

SKILLS IN CONTEXT

GRAMMAR

Adjectives

SKILL TRACE	
Introduce	T46–T47
Review	T69

TEACH/MODEL

Have students identify the adjective and the noun in this phrase: *dangerous beast.* (dangerous; beast) Remind students that an adjective is a word used to describe a noun. Model how adjectives describe nouns.

MODEL **I know that the word *limb* on page 39 is a noun. I see that the adjective *dead* describes the noun *limb*. The adjective *dead* gives more information about the limb and helps me understand what happened in the story. A dead tree limb is brittle and breaks easily.**

PRACTICE/APPLY

Challenge students to find more adjectives on this page and in the rest of the story as they read. Have them create a chart that lists adjectives and the nouns they describe.

Adjectives	Nouns
hungry	babies
timid, little	creature

REACHING ALL LEARNERS

INTERVENTION STRATEGIES

MODIFIED INSTRUCTION Help students summarize what has happened so far. Because the iguana does not want to listen to the mosquito, he puts two sticks in his ears. Since he cannot hear, the iguana doesn't answer the python. The python gets worried and hides in the rabbit's hole. The rabbit runs from the snake. The crow sees the rabbit and sounds an alarm. This makes the monkey leap through the trees and onto a dead limb that falls and kills a baby owl. Mother Owl is so sad she does not wake the sun, and day can't begin.

Then help students set a purpose for reading through page 43. (to find out what the animals will do to get Mother Owl to hoot for the sun)

Monitor Comprehension

1. **How do the illustrators show you that night is lasting longer than it should?** (The background is dark throughout this part of the story.) CRITICAL: ILLUSTRATOR'S CRAFT/INTERPRET VISUAL IMAGERY

2. **How do you know that Monkey is worried when he talks to King Lion?** (He is described as "nervously glancing from side to side") LITERAL: NOTE DETAILS

3. **What does King Lion find out from Mother Owl and the monkey? What do you think will happen next?** (Mother Owl can't bear to wake the sun because the monkey killed one of her owlets; the monkey blames the crow for what happened; predictions will vary.) INFERENTIAL: MAKE PREDICTIONS

Guided Reading

STRATEGIES GOOD READERS USE

FOCUS STRATEGY **Use Text Structure and Format** If students do not guess that King Lion will want to see the crow, remind them that they can use text structure and format to make predictions. Ask these questions:

- **What does Mother Owl tell King Lion?**
- **What does the King do after talking with Mother Owl?**
- **What does the monkey tell King Lion?**
- **Whom will the King probably call next?**

40

CULTURAL CONNECTIONS

COUNCIL MEETING King Lion, chief of the community of forest animals, calls a council meeting to discover why Mother Owl has not called the sun. Council meetings are a traditional method for resolving issues among some African and Native American tribal nations. As in traditional council meetings, all the members of the animal council have a chance to talk before any decisions are made. Ask students to suggest other kinds of councils that meet. (student councils, church councils)

At last King Lion called a meeting of the animals. They came and sat down, pem, pem, pem, around a **council** fire. Mother Owl did not come, so the antelope was sent to fetch her.

When she arrived, King Lion asked, "Mother Owl, why have you not called the sun? The night has lasted long, long, long, and everyone is worried."

Mother Owl said, "Monkey killed one of my owlets. Because of that, I cannot bear to wake the sun."

The king said to the gathered animals:

"Did you hear?
It was the monkey
who killed the owlet —
and now Mother Owl won't wake the sun
so that the day can come."

Then King Lion called the monkey. He came before him nervously glancing from side to side, rim, rim, rim, rim.

"Monkey," said the king, "why did you kill one of Mother Owl's babies?"

"Oh, King," said the monkey, "it was the crow's fault. He was calling and calling to warn us of danger. And I went leaping through the trees to help. A limb broke under me, and it fell taaa on the owl's nest."

The king said to the council:

"So, it was the crow
who alarmed the monkey,
who killed the owlet —
and now Mother Owl won't wake the sun
so that the day can come."

41

ESL

MULTIPLE MEANINGS Remind students that many words in the English language have more than one meaning. Explain that *bear* can be a verb that means "to put up with" or "to deal with." Point out that this is what *bear* means when Mother Owl says *"I cannot bear to wake the sun."* Then explain that *bear* can also be a naming word for a large, furry animal. Invite a volunteer to draw a picture of a bear on the board.

SKILLS IN CONTEXT

DECODING/PHONICS

SKILL TRACE	
Introduce	Grade 2
Maintain	T71

Vowel Variants: /o͞o/*ou, ough*

TEACH/MODEL

Students may have difficulty pronouncing words with the letters *ou* and *ough*. Write these sentences on the board and have volunteers read them aloud:

Did you hear?
And I went leaping through the trees to help.

Ask students to underline the words with the /o͞o/ sound. *(you, through)* Explain that the letters *ou* and *ough* sometimes stand for the /o͞o/ sound that students hear in *you* and *through.*

PRACTICE/APPLY

Write the following sentences on the board:

King Lion spoke to a group of animals.
They came from throughout the forest.

Ask students to read the sentences aloud and identify the words in which they hear the /o͞o/ sound. *(group, throughout)* Have volunteers underline the letters that stand for the /o͞o/ sound in each word. Ask students how knowing that the letters *ou* and *ough* sometimes stand for the /o͞o/ sound can help them read unfamiliar words.

TECHNOLOGY
***PHONICS EXPRESS™ CD-ROM*, Level D Scooter/Route 1/Park and Fire Station**

- ***Phonics Practice Book*, Intermediate, page 167**
- ***Phonics Practice Reader 21***

Monitor Comprehension

1. **What reason does the crow give King Lion for spreading the alarm? Do you agree with the crow that this was "reason enough"?** (Crow says seeing the rabbit run for her life was reason enough to sound the alarm. Maybe the crow should have found out why the rabbit was running before jumping to a conclusion.) CRITICAL: EXPRESS PERSONAL OPINIONS

2. **Why do you think the King agrees with the crow about why he spread an alarm?** (Possible responses: King Lion probably thinks it was strange for Rabbit to be running; Crow was only trying to protect the other animals.) CRITICAL: INTERPRET CHARACTERS' MOTIVATIONS

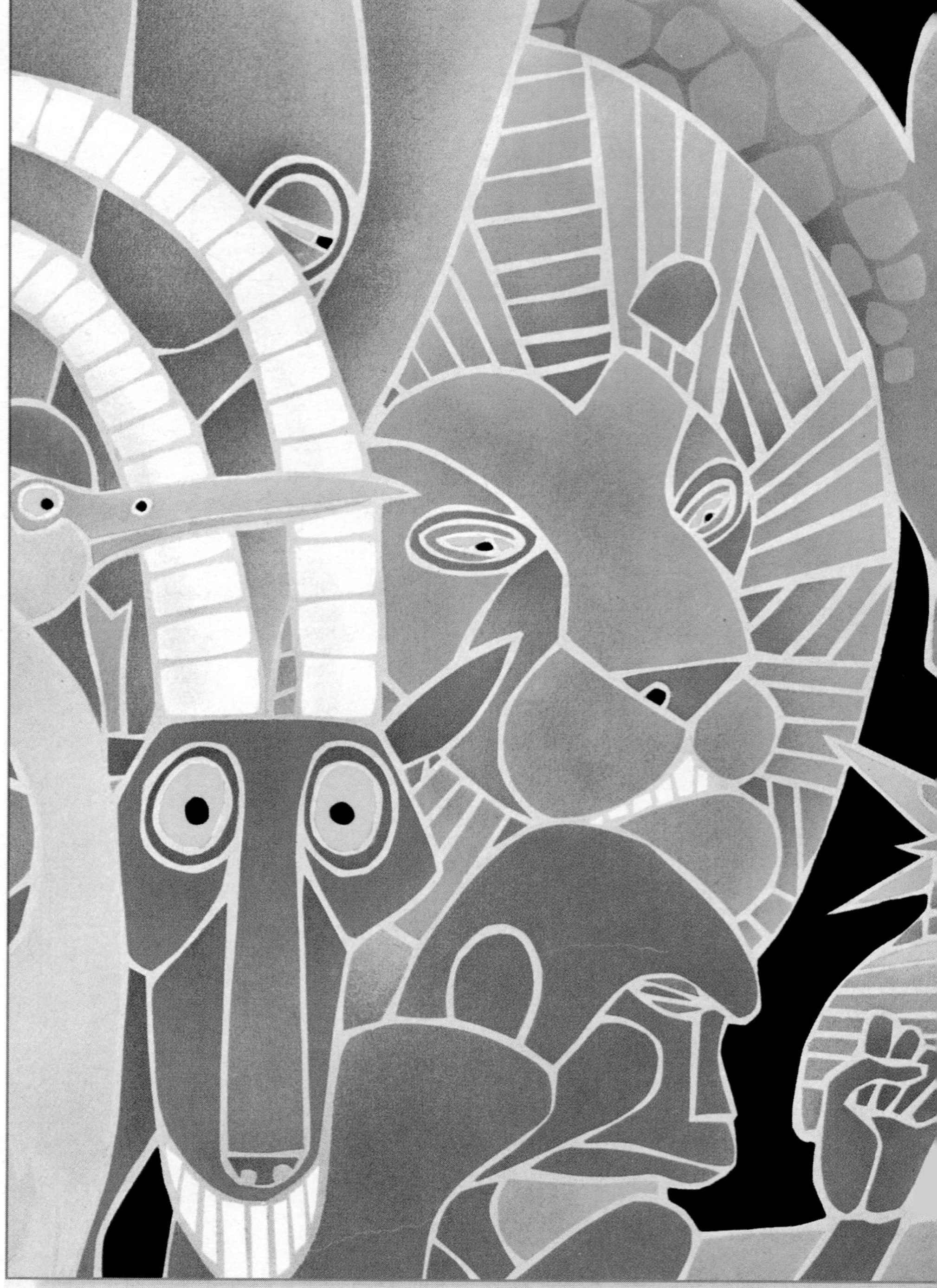

MUSIC

A LADY AND A FLY Some students may be familiar with the classic children's song "There Was an Old Lady Who Swallowed a Fly." This song repeats and builds on previous lines just as the text in this selection does. Invite students who know the song to help teach it to the class. If possible, play a recording of the song so that children may listen and sing along. Some students may enjoy illustrating ideas from the song.

Then the king called for the crow. That big bird came flapping up. He said, "King Lion, it was the rabbit's fault! I saw her running for her life in the daytime. Wasn't that reason enough to spread an alarm?"

The king nodded his head and said to the council:
"So, it was the rabbit
who startled the crow,
who alarmed the monkey,
who killed the owlet —
and now Mother Owl won't wake the sun
so that the day can come."

43

REACHING ALL LEARNERS

INTERVENTION STRATEGIES

MODIFIED INSTRUCTION Help students recall what has happened:

- King Lion has called a council meeting.
- Mother Owl tells King Lion that she cannot bear to wake the sun because the monkey killed her baby.
- The King calls the monkey who tells the King that it was the crow's fault because he was calling to warn the animals of danger.
- Then the King calls the crow, who says it was rabbit's fault because she was running and made him think there was danger.

Then help students set a purpose for reading through page 47. (to find out who else is to blame for the owlet's death)

Monitor Comprehension

1 **How does the way the rabbit acts compare to the way the crow acts? What does that tell you about each character?** (Possible response: The crow comes flapping, but the rabbit is trembling. The crow is bold; the rabbit is timid.) INFERENTIAL: MAKE COMPARISONS/DETERMINE CHARACTERS' TRAITS

2 **What does the King mean when he says the rabbit broke a law of nature?** (Possible response: Rabbits don't usually run around in the day; they usually come out at dusk or dawn.) INFERENTIAL: DRAW CONCLUSIONS

3 **How did knowing about syllables help you read long words on pages 44 and 45?** (Students should explain how they applied syllabication rules to read words like *trembling* and *uncertainly*.) FOCUS SKILL METACOGNITIVE: SYLLABICATION

Guided Reading

STRATEGIES GOOD READERS USE

FOCUS STRATEGY **Use Text Structure and Format** Remind students that they can use text structure and format to summarize and make predictions. Use this think-aloud:

MODEL **As I read, I notice that what happens is very similar to what happened when King Lion called Mother Owl, the monkey, and the crow. Each said it was someone else's fault. I think King Lion will call the python next.**

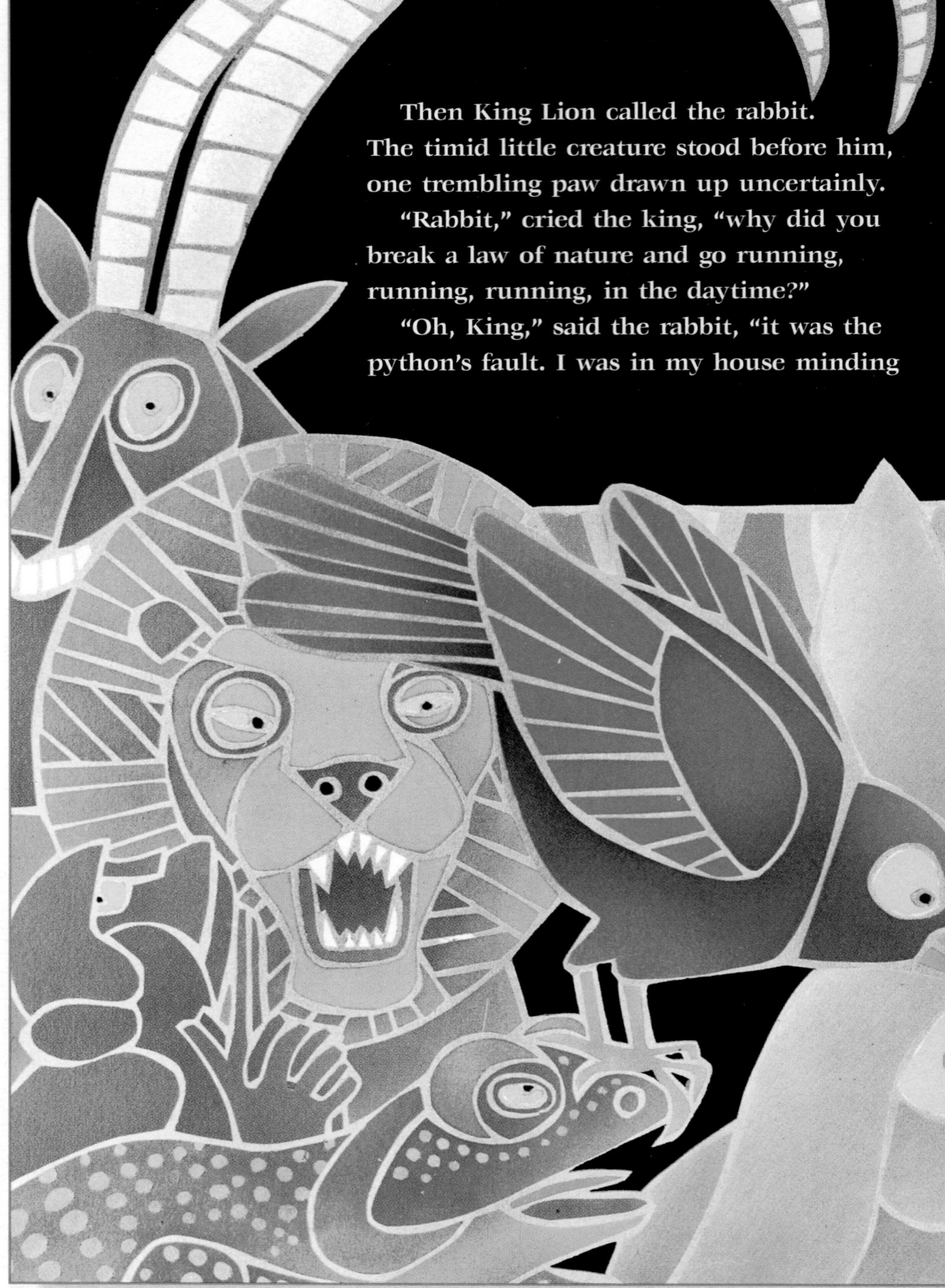

Then King Lion called the rabbit. The timid little creature stood before him, one trembling paw drawn up uncertainly.
"Rabbit," cried the king, "why did you break a law of nature and go running, running, running, in the daytime?"
"Oh, King," said the rabbit, "it was the python's fault. I was in my house minding

ILLUSTRATOR'S CRAFT

ARTISTIC EXPRESSION Have students look at the pictures on pages 44 and 45. Point out the contrast in the expressions of the python, King Lion, and the rabbit. Ask students if they think that the illustrators captured the personality of each of these characters, and have them explain their answers. Ask how students might have drawn the animals if they were illustrating the story.

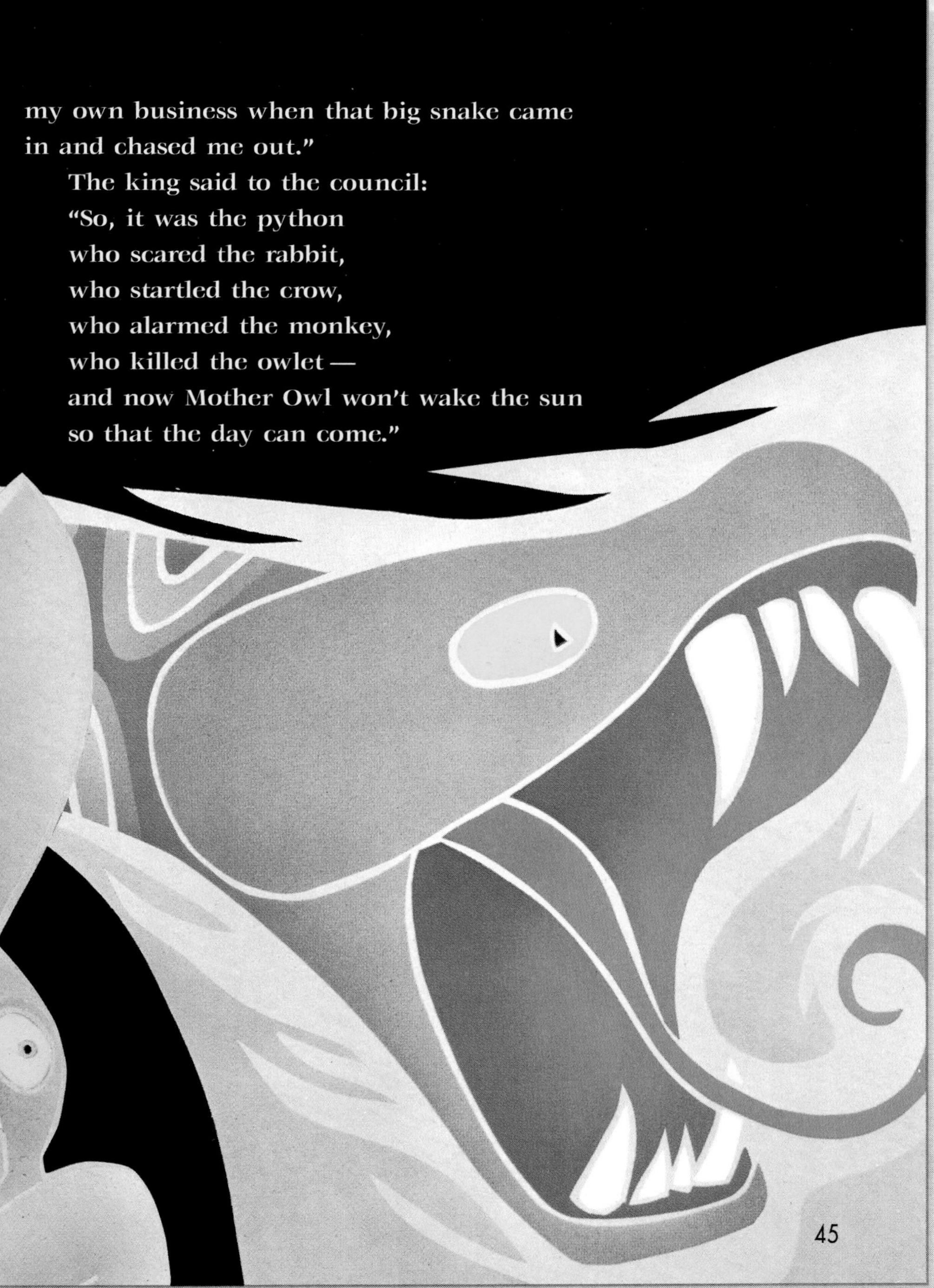

my own business when that big snake came
in and chased me out."
The king said to the council:
"So, it was the python
who scared the rabbit,
who startled the crow,
who alarmed the monkey,
who killed the owlet—
and now Mother Owl won't wake the sun
so that the day can come."
45

SKILLS IN CONTEXT

COMPREHENSION
TESTED SKILL

Sequence

SKILL TRACE	
Introduce	T20, T40
Reteach	R2
Review 1	T75
Review 2	T119
Test	Theme 1
Maintain	T269

TEACH/MODEL

Remind students that knowing the order in which events happen in a story can help readers better understand a story. Ask students what kinds of clues they should look for to figure out time order. (time-order or signal words) Read aloud this sentence and ask students to add *Before, After,* or *Then* to complete it. ______ *Mother Owl told King Lion what happened to her baby, the King called the monkey.* (*After*) Model determining sequence:

MODEL **I know that Mother Owl was the first one to talk to King Lion, so I know King Lion called the monkey after Mother Owl told the King what happened to her baby.**

PRACTICE/APPLY

Help students create a sequence chart.

The mosquito told the iguana a foolish story.
↓
The iguana put sticks in his ears.
↓
The iguana ignored the python.

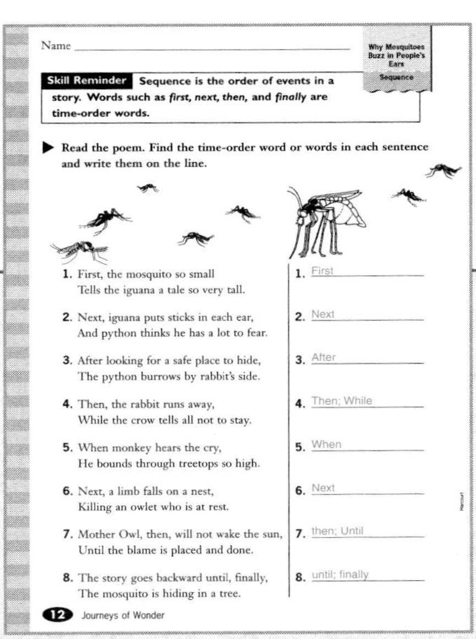
Name ______

Why Mosquitoes Buzz in People's Ears — Sequence

Skill Reminder **Sequence is the order of events in a story. Words such as *first, next, then,* and *finally* are time-order words.**

▶ **Read the poem. Find the time-order word or words in each sentence and write them on the line.**

1. First, the mosquito so small Tells the iguana a tale so very tall.	1. First
2. Next, iguana puts sticks in each ear, And python thinks he has a lot to fear.	2. Next
3. After looking for a safe place to hide, The python burrows by rabbit's side.	3. After
4. Then, the rabbit runs away, While the crow tells all not to stay.	4. Then; While
5. When monkey hears the cry, He bounds through treetops so high.	5. When
6. Next, a limb falls on a nest, Killing an owlet who is at rest.	6. Next
7. Mother Owl, then, will not wake the sun, Until the blame is placed and done.	7. then; Until
8. The story goes backward until, finally, The mosquito is hiding in a tree.	8. until; finally

12 Journeys of Wonder

Harcourt

▲ **Practice Book, page 12**

REACHING ALL LEARNERS

ESL

LAW OF NATURE King Lion says that the rabbit broke a law of nature by running in the daytime. Explain that the rabbit won't get a ticket or go to jail for breaking this law. Tell students that the laws of nature aren't the same kinds of laws that police officers enforce. They are not written down anywhere. "Law of nature" is an expression used to explain the way things usually happen in nature. Invite students to suggest other laws of nature.

Monitor Comprehension

1. **Did it surprise you that King Lion called the python? Why or why not?** (Possible response: No, because the rabbit said that it was the python's fault; it follows the pattern of the text for the King to then call whoever gets blamed.) FOCUS STRATEGY INFERENTIAL: TEXT STRUCTURE

2. **Would a rabbit and a python be friends in real life?** (Possible response: They would not be friends because in real life pythons might eat rabbits.) CRITICAL: DISTINGUISH BETWEEN FANTASY AND REALITY

WORD ASSOCIATION

ANIMALS IN MOTION The verb *slithering* makes us think of a snake and the gliding motion that it makes as it moves. Encourage students to create a word wall of animal names and words that describe how they move. Tell them to begin by looking through the story for examples.

Animal Names	Words for Actions
snake	slithering
rabbit	scurried
crow	flapping
monkey	leaping, swinging

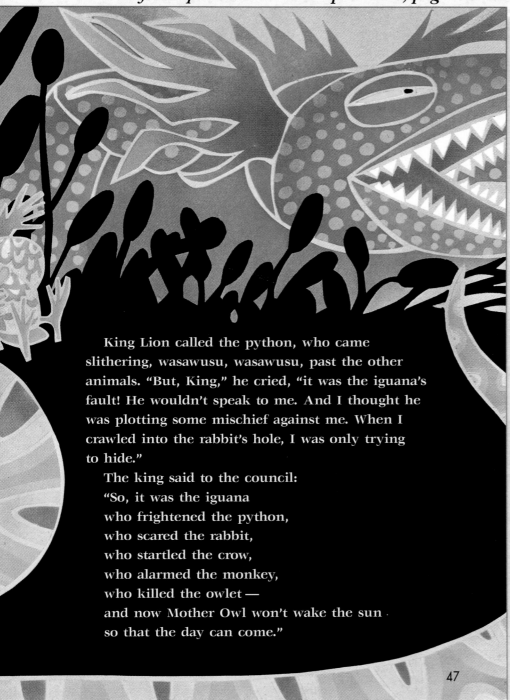

King Lion called the python, who came slithering, wasawusu, wasawusu, past the other animals. "But, King," he cried, "it was the iguana's fault! He wouldn't speak to me. And I thought he was plotting some mischief against me. When I crawled into the rabbit's hole, I was only trying to hide."

The king said to the council:
"So, it was the iguana
who frightened the python,
who scared the rabbit,
who startled the crow,
who alarmed the monkey,
who killed the owlet —
and now Mother Owl won't wake the sun
so that the day can come."

47

Informal Assessment

FOCUS SKILL **SYLLABICATION** To assess whether students are using syllabication to read unfamiliar long words, point out the words *slithering, plotting,* and *frightened* on page 47 and ask questions like the following:

1. What do you know about reading long words by breaking the words up by vowel sounds?
2. What do you know about breaking up words with double consonants into parts to read the words?
3. What do you know about looking for familiar word parts to read long words?

INTERVENTION STRATEGIES

MODIFIED INSTRUCTION Help students summarize what has happened since the King spoke to the crow. King Lion calls the rabbit, who says that the python scared her when he came into her hole, which is why she was running during the day. Then the python explains that he went into the hole because he thought the iguana was plotting some mischief against him. Help students set a purpose for reading through page 51. (to find out who really is to blame for the owlet's death and if Mother Owl will finally call the sun so the day will come)

Monitor Comprehension

1 **Why didn't the iguana hear the summons to attend the council meeting?** (Possible response: because he still had the sticks in his ears and couldn't hear anything) INFERENTIAL: DRAW CONCLUSIONS

2 **How would you describe the iguana's reaction when King Lion asks what evil he's been plotting? Why do you think he reacts this way?** (Possible response: surprised; he has no idea what has been going on because he's had the sticks in his ears) INFERENTIAL: DETERMINE CHARACTERS' EMOTIONS

Guided Reading

STRATEGIES GOOD READERS USE

Self-Question If students have trouble understanding the iguana's reaction to what is happening, they may have forgotten what happened earlier in the story. Remind them to ask themselves questions to check their comprehension. Use these prompts:

- **What did the iguana do so that he wouldn't have to listen to the mosquito?**
- **What else did the iguana not hear?**

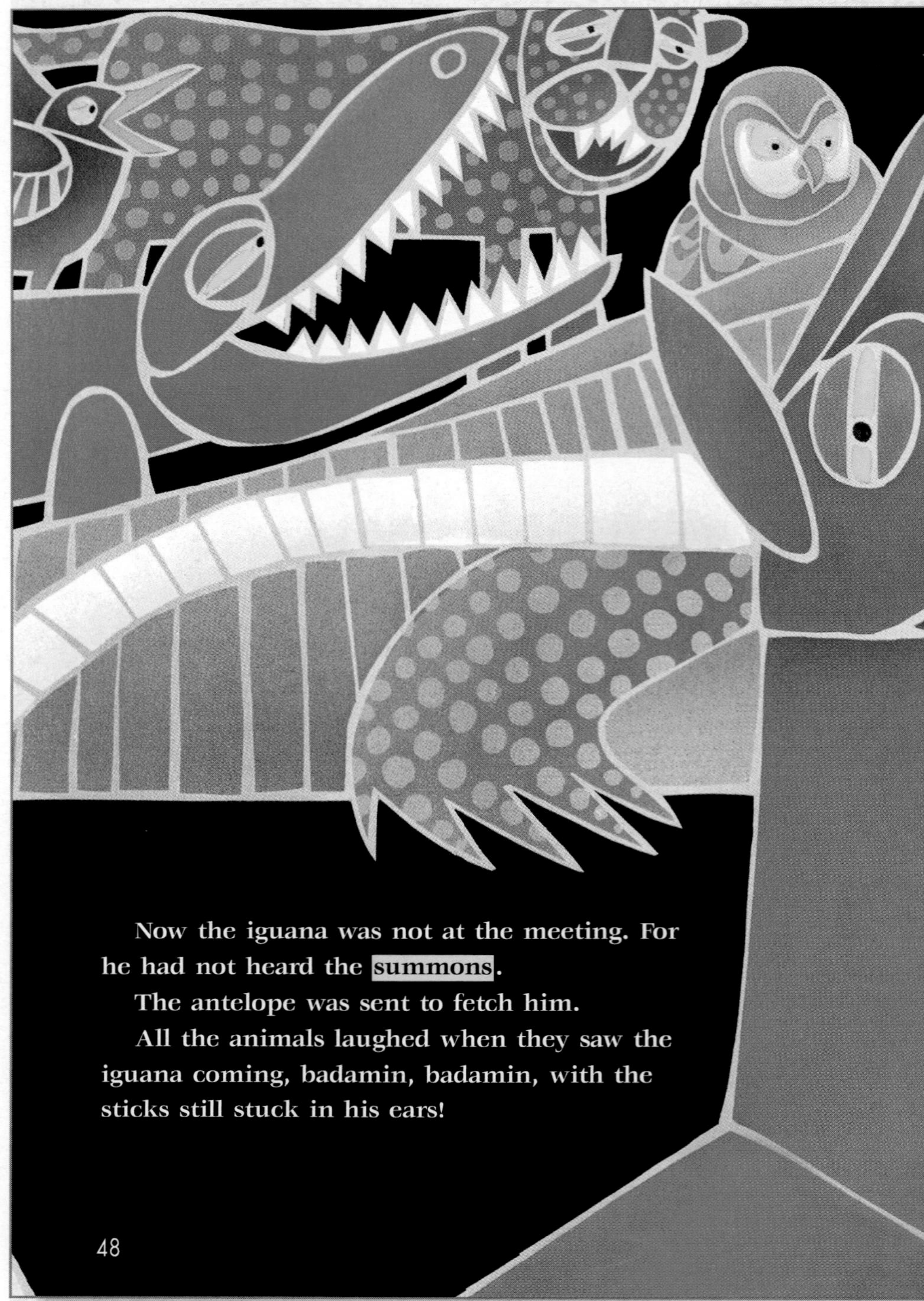

Now the iguana was not at the meeting. For he had not heard the summons.

The antelope was sent to fetch him.

All the animals laughed when they saw the iguana coming, badamin, badamin, with the sticks still stuck in his ears!

48

WORD STUDY

TONGUE TWISTERS Tell students to listen for repeated sounds as you read aloud the last paragraph on page 48. Emphasize the sounds at the beginning of *sticks still stuck*. Then encourage students to create tongue twisters about the story. They can use *sticks still stuck* and add other *st* words, or they can use different beginning sounds. Invite students to share their tongue twisters with the class.

Stop staring at the sticks still stuck in my ears.

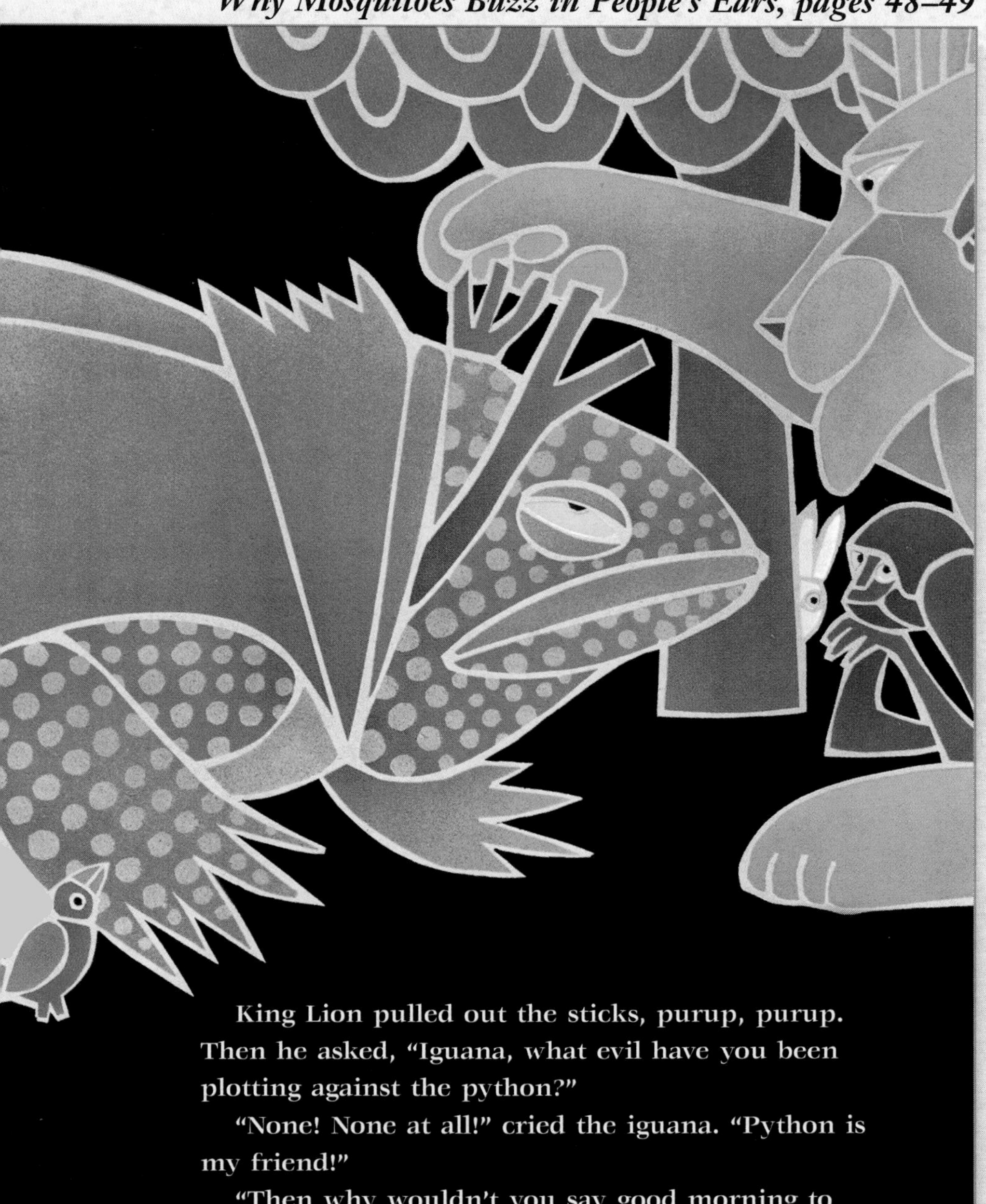

King Lion pulled out the sticks, purup, purup. Then he asked, "Iguana, what evil have you been plotting against the python?"

"None! None at all!" cried the iguana. "Python is my friend!"

"Then why wouldn't you say good morning to me?" demanded the snake.

49

CHALLENGE

USING ILLUSTRATIONS TO EXPAND COMPREHENSION Have students examine the illustrations on pages 48 and 49. Invite them to describe what they see in the illustrations and to explain how the illustrations add to their understanding of the characters and their appreciation of the story.

Monitor Comprehension

1. **If you were King Lion, what might you have said to the iguana when you heard his story about the mosquito?** (Possible response: The King should have pointed out to the iguana that if he hadn't stuck the sticks in his ears, none of this would have happened.) METACOGNITIVE: MAKE JUDGMENTS

2. **What made Mother Owl hoot for the sun?** (Possible response: She was satisfied that the whole truth was finally uncovered and that the mosquito would be punished.) INFERENTIAL: CAUSE-EFFECT

3. **What do you think will happen to the mosquito?** (Possible response: He might get called before the council and be punished.) INFERENTIAL: MAKE PREDICTIONS

4. **What lesson do you think this story teaches?** (Possible responses: Don't jump to conclusions; think before you act.) CRITICAL: INTERPRET THEME

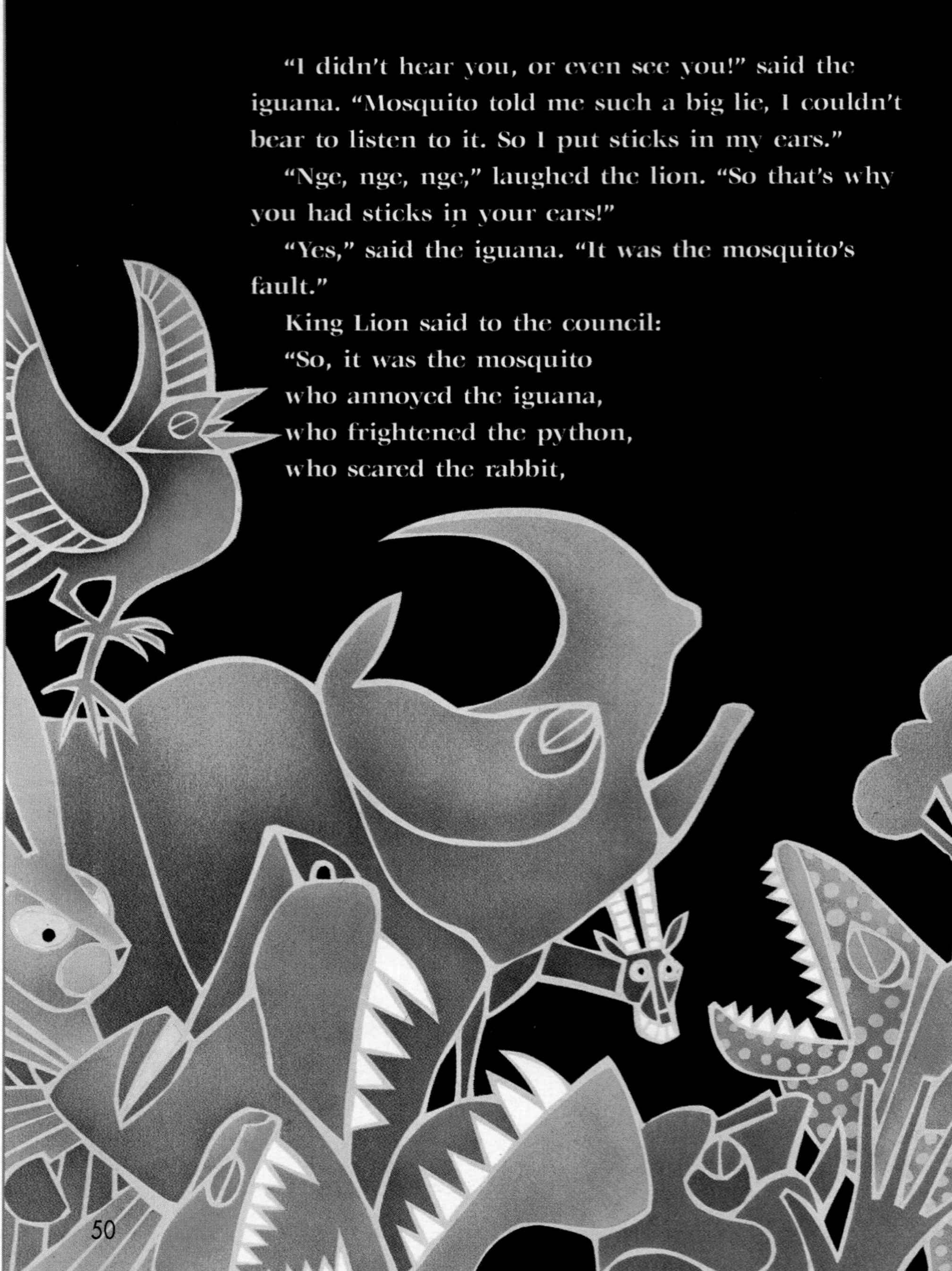

"I didn't hear you, or even see you!" said the iguana. "Mosquito told me such a big lie, I couldn't bear to listen to it. So I put sticks in my ears."

"Nge, nge, nge," laughed the lion. "So that's why you had sticks in your ears!"

"Yes," said the iguana. "It was the mosquito's fault."

King Lion said to the council:
"So, it was the mosquito
who annoyed the iguana,
who frightened the python,
who scared the rabbit,

50

ART

CREATE A MURAL Encourage students to reread King Lion's refrain that begins, "So it was the mosquito . . ." and ends ". . . so the day can come." Tell them to create a mental image of what he is describing. Then have students work in groups to create a mural that illustrates the refrain.

who startled the crow,
who alarmed the monkey,
who killed the owlet—
and now Mother Owl won't wake the sun
so that the day can come."

"Punish the mosquito! Punish the mosquito!" cried all the animals.

When Mother Owl heard that, she was satisfied. She turned her head toward the east and hooted: "Hoo! Hooooo! Hoooooooo!"

And the sun came up.

51

REACHING ALL LEARNERS

INTERVENTION STRATEGIES

MODIFIED INSTRUCTION Help students summarize the chain of events that led to the owlet's death:

- Because he does not want to listen to mosquito's lie, the iguana puts sticks in his ears and cannot hear the python's greeting.
- The python is frightened and scares the rabbit, who alarms the crow, who startles the monkey, who leaps on a branch that falls and kills the owlet.
- Mother Owl is sad, and so she will not hoot for the sun to rise.
- At a council meeting, King Lion uncovers what has happened.

Literary Response

RETURN TO THE PREDICTIONS/PURPOSE

Were your predictions about this story confirmed? Discuss with students whether their purpose for reading was met.

APPRECIATING THE LITERATURE

Did you like the way the author repeated words and phrases in the story? Why or why not? (Responses will vary.)

Think About It

1. **How did the iguana's actions cause Mother Owl not to wake the sun?** (He started a series of events that killed one of her owlets and made her sad. Students should be able to retell the series of events.) INFERENTIAL: SUMMARIZE/THEME CONNECTIONS
2. **What would you have done differently if the mosquito had told you the yam story?** (Possible responses: walked away; told the mosquito not to tell lies) CRITICAL: MAKE JUDGMENTS/PERSONAL RESPONSE
3. **What kind of tale is this? Why do you think it is still being told today?** (Possible responses: a folktale; it is still being told because it is entertaining and teaches an important lesson) CRITICAL: LITERARY ANALYSIS

Meanwhile the mosquito had listened to it all from a nearby bush. She crept under a curly leaf, semm, and was never found and brought before the council.

But because of this the mosquito has a guilty conscience. To this day she goes about whining in people's ears: "Zeee! Is everyone still angry at me?"

When she does that, she gets an honest answer.

THINK ABOUT IT

1. How did the iguana's actions cause Mother Owl not to wake the sun?
2. What would you have done differently if the mosquito had told you the yam story?
3. What kind of tale is this? Why do you think it is still being told today?

Informal Assessment

RETELL

Have each student retell the story in his or her own words. Check whether the student

- ☐ gives the main idea and relevant details in sequence.
- ☐ uses vocabulary from the text.
- ☐ is able to evaluate and appreciate the author's use of language in creating the text.
- ☐ understands cause-effect relationships in the text.

SUMMARIZE

Encourage students to summarize the story by recalling the characters' actions. Students can refer to the character chart they completed while reading. See also *Practice Book* page 13.

ONE-SENTENCE SUMMARY Have students use their completed character charts to write a one-sentence summary of the folktale.

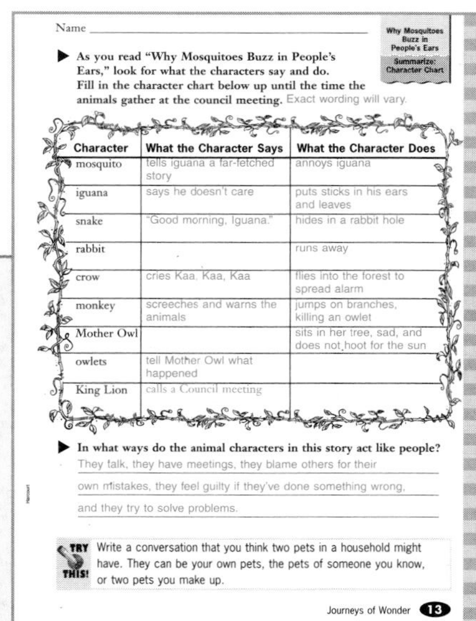

Name ______

Why Mosquitoes Buzz in People's Ears
Summarize: Character Chart

▶ **As you read "Why Mosquitoes Buzz in People's Ears," look for what the characters say and do. Fill in the character chart below up until the time the animals gather at the council meeting.** Exact wording will vary.

Character	What the Character Says	What the Character Does
mosquito	tells iguana a far-fetched story	annoys iguana
iguana	says he doesn't care	puts sticks in his ears and leaves
snake	"Good morning, Iguana."	hides in a rabbit hole
rabbit		runs away
crow	cries Kaa, Kaa, Kaa	flies into the forest to spread alarm
monkey	screeches and warns the animals	jumps on branches, killing an owlet
Mother Owl		sits in her tree, sad, and does not hoot for the sun
owlets	tell Mother Owl what happened	
King Lion	calls a Council meeting	

▶ **In what ways do the animal characters in this story act like people?**

They talk, they have meetings, they blame others for their own mistakes, they feel guilty if they've done something wrong, and they try to solve problems.

TRY THIS! Write a conversation that you think two pets in a household might have. They can be your own pets, the pets of someone you know, or two pets you make up.

Journeys of Wonder 13

▲ **Practice Book, page 13**

MEET THE ILLUSTRATORS

LEO AND DIANE DILLON

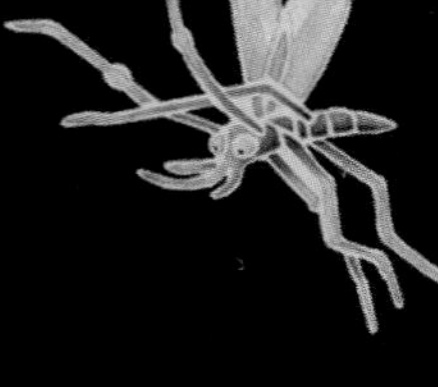

Leo and Diane Dillon have been working as a team for more than thirty years! They are married and work in New York City. But what did they do before they were a team?

When Leo Dillon was a boy, he drew pictures of everything he saw. Although his parents encouraged him to draw, they hoped he would become a lawyer or doctor. Unlike her husband, Diane Dillon didn't always want to be an artist. She thought about becoming a nurse. After taking a few art lessons, she decided to go to art school. That is where she met Leo Dillon.

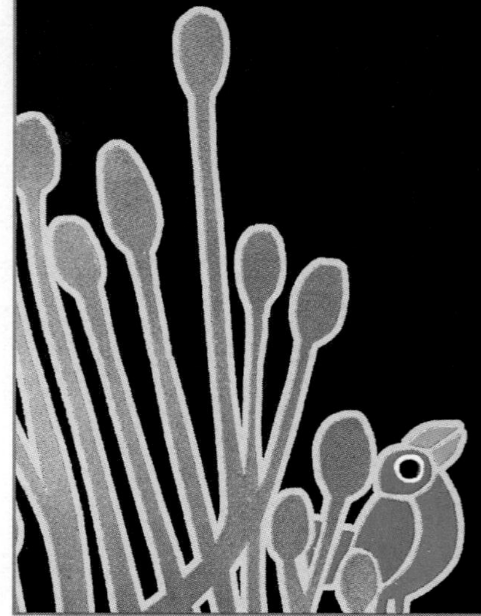

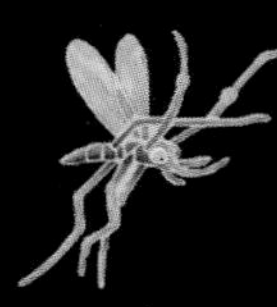

The Dillons have worked together on book covers, magazines, posters, and children's books. When working on a picture together, they pass the drawing back and forth between them. They each draw one small section at a time. Their work has won them many awards, including two Caldecott Medals in a row!

Leo Dillon

Diane Dillon

Visit *The Learning Site!*
www.harcourtschool.com

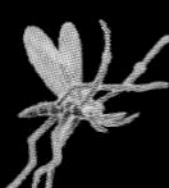

55

My Notes

ABOUT THE ILLUSTRATORS

LEO AND DIANE DILLON say that their method of working so closely creates what they call "a third artist." In this way, they say, "we are able to create art we would not be able to do individually."

Discuss why the Dillons might choose to work as a team. Then ask students to examine the illustrations in the text closely to see if they can tell that two different artists worked on a drawing. Ask what problems might arise when two different artists are working on one drawing. (Possible response: The artists may have different ideas about how to illustrate a book.)

INTERNET Additional author information can be found on *The Learning Site* at **www.harcourtschool.com**

Companion Selection

INTRODUCE THE FABLE

Ask students to recall the crow's duty in "Why Mosquitoes Buzz in People's Ears." (to spread the alarm in case of danger) Point out that the crow tries to help the other animals. Then tell students that they are going to read a fable called "The Ant and the Dove" in which one animal helps another. Remind them that a fable usually has a moral in it, or a lesson to be learned.

APPRECIATING THE FABLE

Suggest that students read the fable silently to find out how the ant and the dove help each other. Then reread the fable aloud to students, and ask the following questions:

1. **Why does the ant sting the hunter?** (Possible response: to save the dove) **Why would the ant want to help the dove?** (Possible response: because the dove had saved the ant from drowning) INFERENTIAL: CAUSE-EFFECT

2. **Are the last three lines important to the fable? Why or why not?** (Possible response: yes, because they express the main idea or the moral of the story) CRITICAL: MAKE JUDGMENTS

REREADING FOR A PURPOSE

This fable is written in verse. Have two groups of students alternate reading couplets (two lines) aloud through "the hunter ran away." Then have both groups together read the last three sentences. Have students identify pairs of rhyming words. (*down, drown; hand, land; prey, away; brother, another*)

▼ FABLE

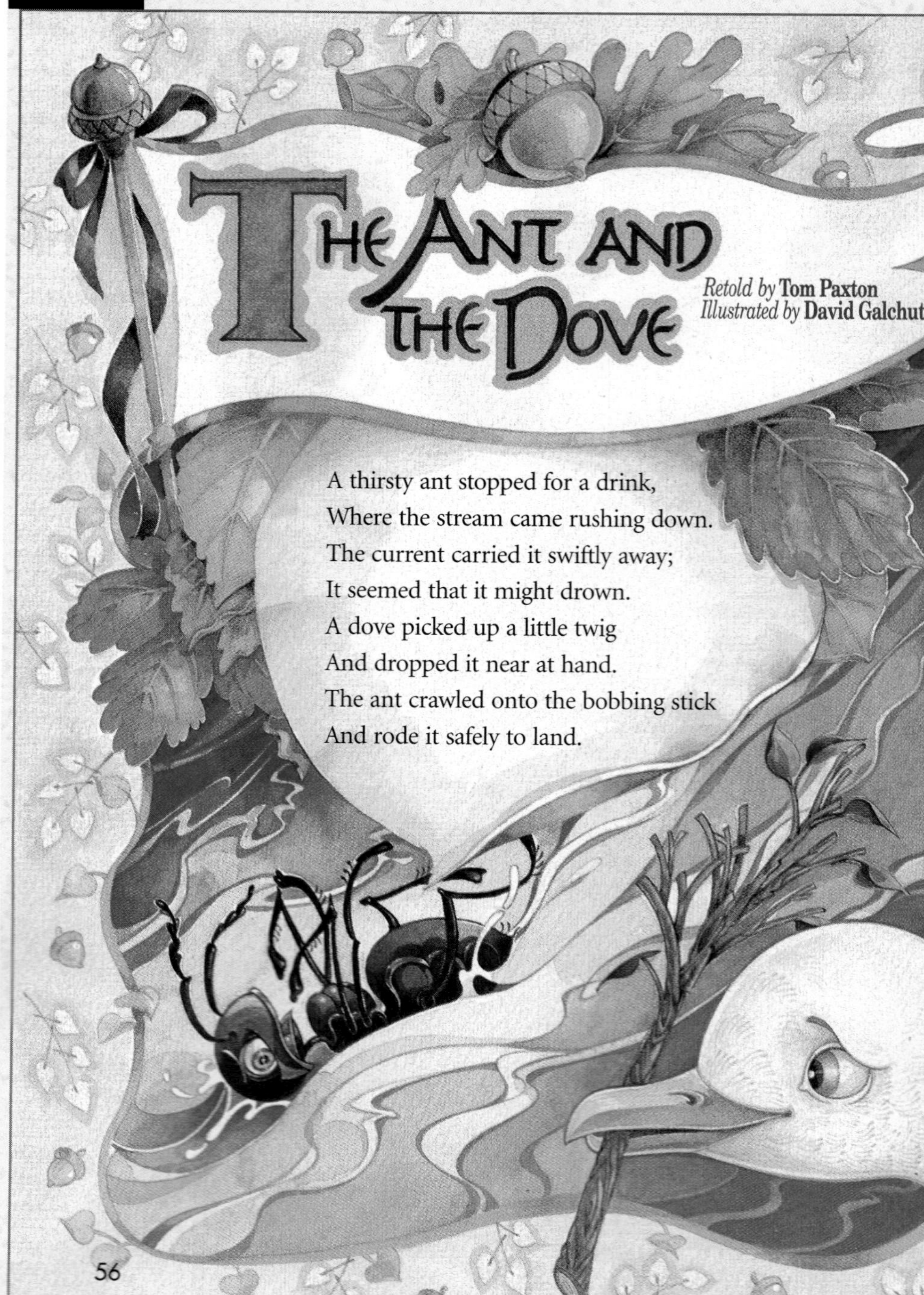

The Ant and the Dove
Retold by Tom Paxton
Illustrated by David Galchutt
A thirsty ant stopped for a drink,
Where the stream came rushing down.
The current carried it swiftly away;
It seemed that it might drown.
A dove picked up a little twig
And dropped it near at hand.
The ant crawled onto the bobbing stick
And rode it safely to land.
56

COMPARING TEXTS

Discuss with students some of the differences between "The Ant and the Dove" and "Why Mosquitoes Buzz in People's Ears." Students can complete a diagram like the one below to show the similarities and differences.

"The Ant and the Dove"
—animals help each other
—involves a human

—involve animals
—teach lessons

"Why Mosquitoes Buzz in People's Ears"
—one animal hurts another
—takes place in the forest

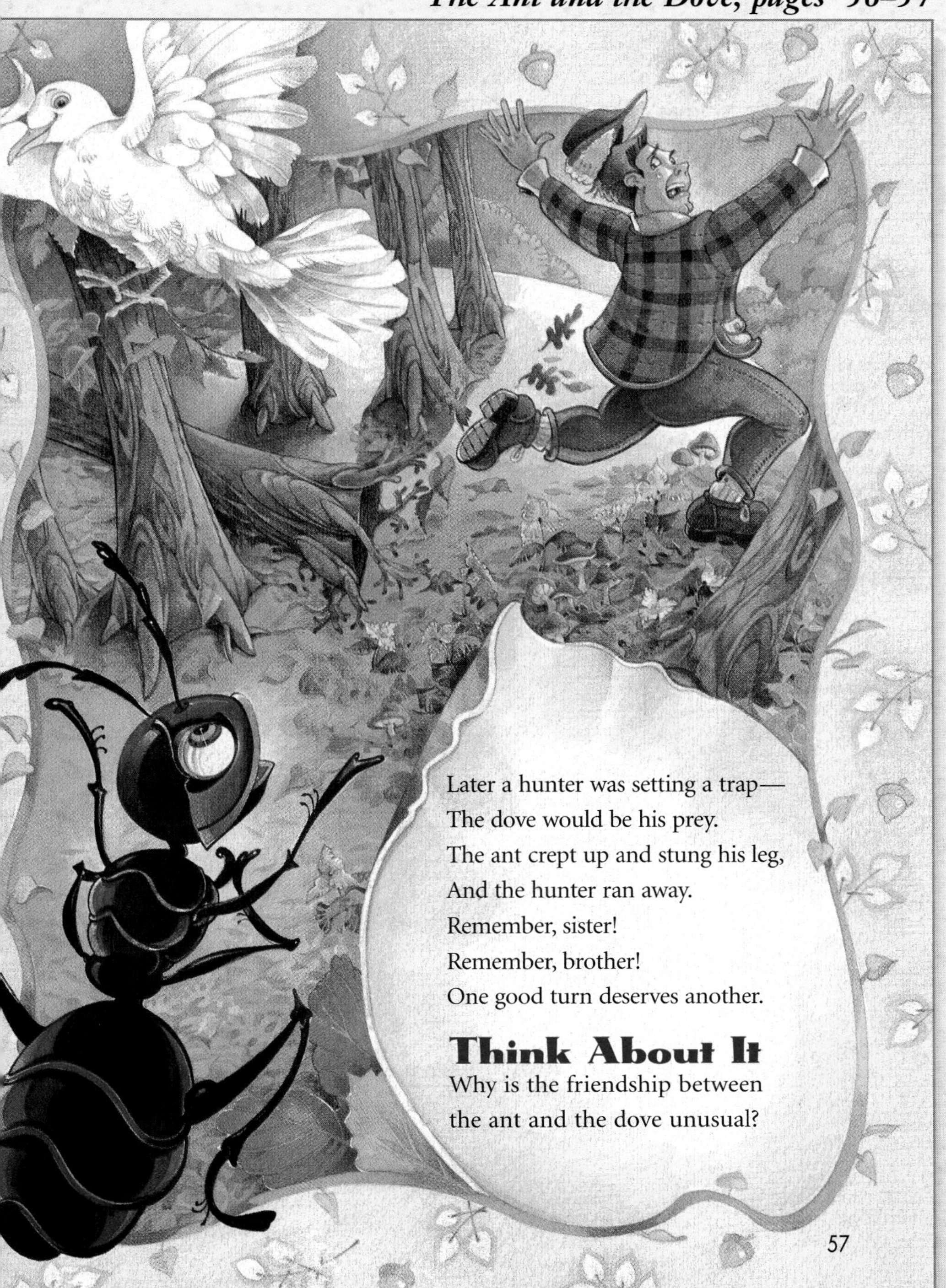

Later a hunter was setting a trap—
The dove would be his prey.
The ant crept up and stung his leg,
And the hunter ran away.
Remember, sister!
Remember, brother!
One good turn deserves another.
Think About It
Why is the friendship between
the ant and the dove unusual?
57

ABOUT THE AUTHOR

Aesop lived in Greece in the 6th century B.C. No one is sure about how much Aesop wrote. Many people believe he is the author of a collection of animal fables that teach lessons. These fables were passed down orally for a long period of time before they were finally written down by Greek and Roman writers. Have students compare and contrast "The Ant and the Dove" to traditional stories that teach lessons from other cultures. Have them illustrate the theme of each story.

Activity Choices

MOSQUITO SPEAKS

Tell a Story Engage students in a discussion of what it feels like to be blamed for something when you may or may not be at fault. Students can draw on these feelings as they tell mosquito's story. CRITICAL: ANALYZE CHARACTERS

HERE'S WHY

Create a Pourquoi Tale Invite students to take turns asking *why* questions about nature. List ideas on the board. Students can then refer to the list for story ideas. Provide time for students to rehearse their stories. CREATIVE: PRESENT PRODUCTIONS

WEST AFRICA TODAY

Write a Report Provide atlases, books, and magazines on West Africa for students to use as references. Students may wish to make displays about West Africa. Displays and reports can be put in the library. CRITICAL: USE MULTIPLE SOURCES/ ORGANIZE INFORMATION

MAKING CONNECTIONS

Write a Story Suggest that groups of three students take the roles of the ant, the dove, and the mosquito, and talk about what happened to them in the story and in the fable. Students can use ideas generated in the group discussion to write their stories. CREATIVE: WRITING/MAKE THEME CONNECTIONS

RESPONSE ACTIVITIES

MOSQUITO SPEAKS

TELL A STORY

Imagine that you are Mosquito, and retell the story your way. Explain why you said what you did about the yams, and tell what happened next. Was it fair that you got all the blame?

HERE'S WHY

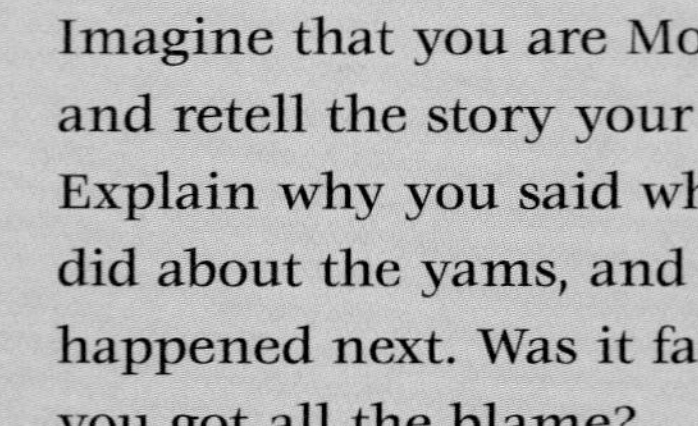

CREATE A POURQUOI TALE

The French word *pourquoi* means "why." This story explains why mosquitoes buzz in people's ears. Make up a story that explains something else. You might tell why tigers have stripes, why crickets chirp, or why moles live underground. Then act out your story with some classmates.

58

SCHOOL-HOME CONNECTION

Suggest that students work with family members to complete the activities on the copying master on page R19. You may wish to assign some or all of the activities as homework during the week.

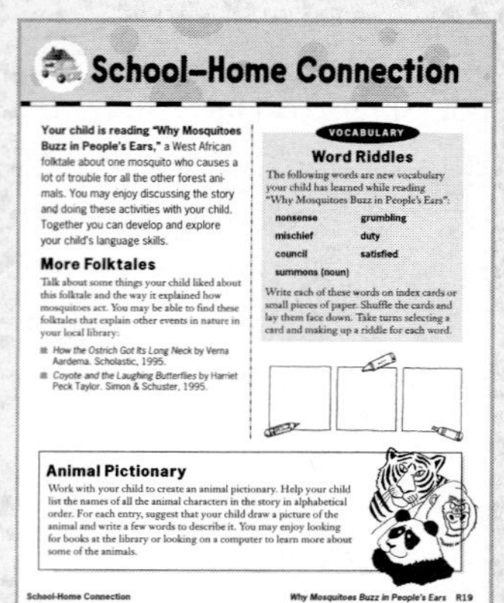

School–Home Connection

Your child is reading "Why Mosquitoes Buzz in People's Ears," a West African folktale about one mosquito who causes a lot of trouble for all the other forest animals. You may enjoy discussing the story and doing these activities with your child. Together you can develop and explore your child's language skills.

More Folktales

Talk about some things your child liked about this folktale and the way it explained how mosquitoes act. You may be able to find these folktales that explain other events in nature in your local library:

- *How the Ostrich Got Its Long Neck* by Verna Aardema. Scholastic, 1995.
- *Coyote and the Laughing Butterflies* by Harriet Peck Taylor. Simon & Schuster, 1995.

VOCABULARY

Word Riddles

The following words are new vocabulary your child has learned while reading "Why Mosquitoes Buzz in People's Ears":

nonsense **grumbling**
mischief **duty**
council **satisfied**
summons (noun)

Write each of these words on index cards or small pieces of paper. Shuffle the cards and lay them face down. Take turns selecting a card and making up a riddle for each word.

Animal Pictionary

Work with your child to create an animal pictionary. Help your child list the names of all the animal characters in the story in alphabetical order. For each entry, suggest that your child draw a picture of the animal and write a few words to describe it. You may enjoy looking for books at the library or looking on a computer to learn more about some of the animals.

School-Home Connection — *Why Mosquitoes Buzz in People's Ears* R19

Copying Master, p. R19 ▶

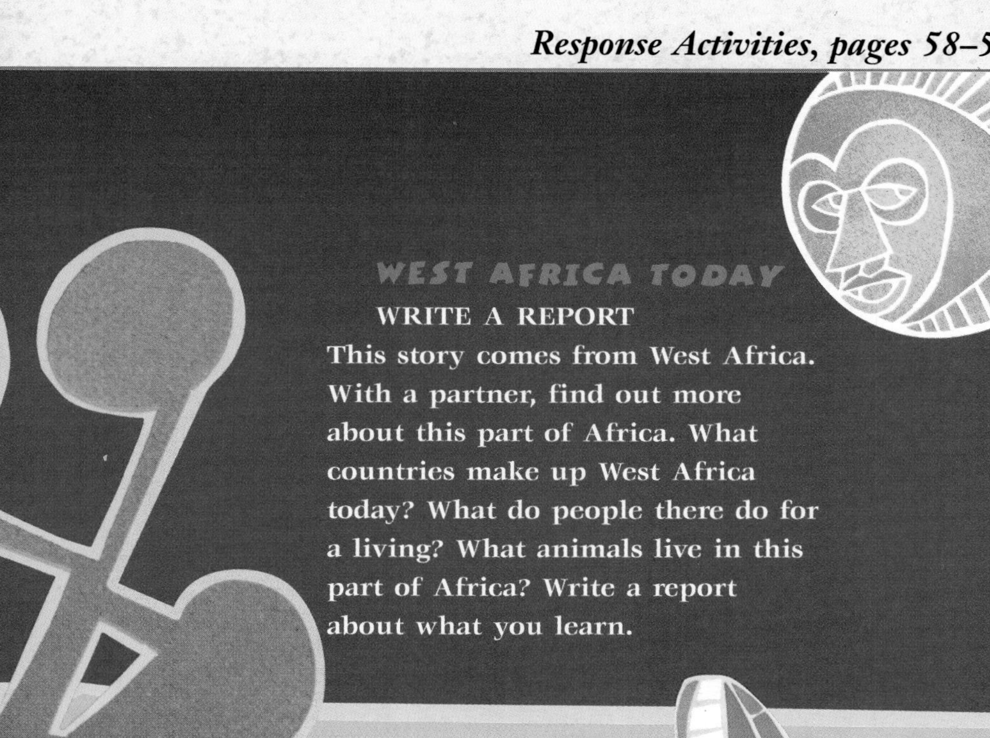

WEST AFRICA TODAY

WRITE A REPORT

This story comes from West Africa. With a partner, find out more about this part of Africa. What countries make up West Africa today? What do people there do for a living? What animals live in this part of Africa? Write a report about what you learn.

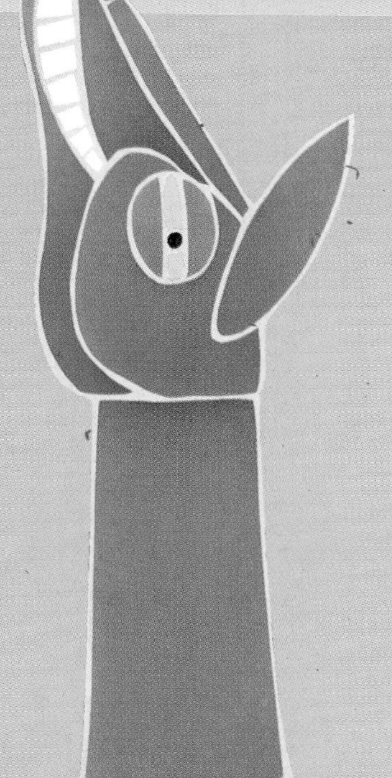

MAKING CONNECTIONS

WRITE A STORY

What if the ant and the dove met the mosquito from "Why Mosquitoes Buzz in People's Ears"? What would they say to each other? Write a new story. Tell what the ant and the dove might say to the mosquito about how to treat others.

INTERVENTION STRATEGIES

MAKING CONNECTIONS In the Making Connections activity, some students may need help understanding the characters so that they can figure out what these characters might say to each other. Provide this chart for them to use:

Character	What the character does and says	What might the character do and say in my story
mosquito (page 35, 52) dove (page 56) ant (page 57)		

Assessment

SELECTION COMPREHENSION TEST

To evaluate comprehension, see pages 4–6.

INFORMAL ASSESSMENT

PERFORMANCE ASSESSMENT Student work for the Making Connections activity may be used for performance assessment of story comprehension.

PORTFOLIO OPPORTUNITY

Students may want to add their West Africa Today reports to their portfolios.

Building Literacy Skills

REREADING FOR FLUENCY

Readers Theatre

Divide students into two groups for a two-part Readers Theatre presentation of the story. The first group can present up to the point where Mother Owl learns her baby is dead, and the second group can present the part about the meeting. You may wish to assign the role of King Lion to two or three students. Suggest that students think of appropriate gestures and movements. They should practice reading until they can read fluently and automatically. LISTENING/SPEAKING/READING

WRITING

A Summons

Have students brainstorm what King Lion might put in a written summons to the animals. Remind students that a summons is an order for someone to appear and not just a friendly invitation. Students can then write an official summons to a character of their choice. Have them refer to the writing tips on Activity Card 33, page R14, for help.

LISTENING/SPEAKING/WRITING

Activity Card 33 ▶

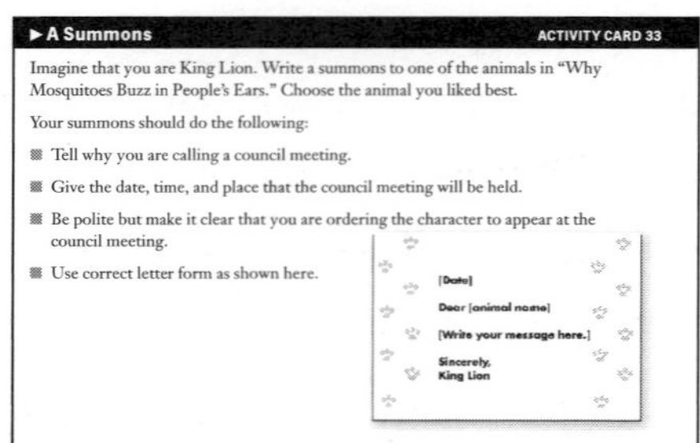

▶ A Summons ACTIVITY CARD 33

Imagine that you are King Lion. Write a summons to one of the animals in "Why Mosquitoes Buzz in People's Ears." Choose the animal you liked best.

Your summons should do the following:

- Tell why you are calling a council meeting.
- Give the date, time, and place that the council meeting will be held.
- Be polite but make it clear that you are ordering the character to appear at the council meeting.
- Use correct letter form as shown here.

[Date]

Dear [animal name]

[Write your message here.]

Sincerely,
King Lion

ORAL LANGUAGE

A Debate

Have students work in two groups—one that agrees with the idea of having a council meeting, and one that thinks the lion should have just ordered the owl to hoot for the sun. The two groups can debate the value of the council meeting in dealing with conflicts. LISTENING/SPEAKING

Remind speakers to

- use standard grammar, including subject-verb agreement and correct tense.
- state valid reasons to support their opinions.

Remind listeners to

- take notes about the arguments and form their own opinions.
- retell the speaker's message afterward to summarize and clarify.

VIEWING

Cut-out Designs

The illustrators for "Why Mosquitoes Buzz in People's Ears" achieved the cut-out look of the designs by using a stencil cut from tracing paper to color one part of the drawing at a time, while keeping the other parts covered. Have students study the designs used in the animal images in the selection. Then have them create their own cut designs and use the cut-outs to decorate or create an animal figure.

VIEWING/REPRESENTING

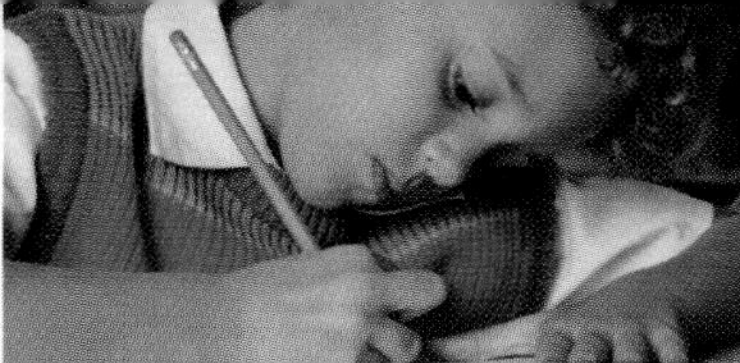

Intervention Strategies for Below-Level Readers

REREADING

Reinforce Comprehension

FOCUS STRATEGY **Apply the focus strategy.** Remind students that reading strategies can help them increase their understanding of what they read. The focus strategy for reading "Why Mosquitoes Buzz in People's Ears" is Use Text Structure and Format. Discuss the strategy with students by asking questions such as these:

- **How can noticing the way text is placed on a page help you while you read a story?**
- **How does recognizing repeated words and phrases in the story help you understand patterns in the plot?**

Have students practice using this strategy. As they silently reread pages 41, 43, 44–45, 47, and 50–51, have them use a chart like the one below to note where they find repeated patterns in the plot and the repetition of words, phrases, and text structure.

Page Numbers	41	43	44-45	47	50-51
Repeated pattern The animal blames a different animal.	X	X	X	X	X
Repeated phrase "The King said to the council..."	X	X	X	X	X
Repeated text structure—a list Lion's list that begins "So, it was the..."	X	X	X	X	X

LANGUAGE EXPLORATION

Explore Idioms

Discuss idioms. Write the phrase *helping out* on the board. Mention that the word *out* in this phrase does not mean "outside"; explain that this phrase is an *idiom*, an expression that has a different meaning than the words by themselves. Help students generate a list to record idioms in which the word *out* is used. Model using these expressions in speech, and have students use them. Discuss why each pair of words go together. Ask whether the words mean the same things together as they do separately.

Guide students in using each pair of words in an oral sentence. Model using each word pair as necessary. Students may enjoy illustrating other idioms they are familiar with, such as *elbow grease*.

out
finding out
cleaning out
watching out
looking out
running out
throwing out
pointing out

EXTENDING SKILLS &
STRATEGIES

FOCUS SKILL Syllabication

AFTER READING

SKILL TRACE	
Introduce	
• Before Reading:	T60–T61
• During Reading:	T66, T74
• After Reading:	T92–T93
Reteach	R3
Review	T273

OBJECTIVE:

To use syllabication to read unfamiliar words

REACHING ALL LEARNERS

ESL

Students can practice using syllabication by drawing vertical lines between the syllables in the following words: *tomorrow, vacation, holiday*, and *calendar*. Remind students that each syllable should have a vowel sound.

INTERVENTION

Help students find long words in an article from a wildlife magazine or a science textbook and use the skill to decode them.

RETEACH See page R3 for a lesson in multiple modalities.

Return to the Concept

Extend the thinking. Remind students that they can decode long unfamiliar words by breaking the words into smaller parts, or syllables. If necessary, help them recall that a syllable is a word part with one vowel sound. Review the Tips for Reading Long Words on Transparency 8. Then invite volunteers to explain the syllabication rules they used to read any of the following words in "Why Mosquitoes Buzz in People's Ears." Page numbers indicate where each word appears in the story.

Point out the tip about accenting the first syllable in two-syllable words. Explain that there are times when the accent is shifted to the second syllable, and when that happens, the meaning of the word can change. Use *present* as an example. Have volunteers suggest sentences using the two different pronunciations of the word.

Model using syllabication rules. Have students find the word *annoyed* on page 50 of the story. Model how to apply syllabication rules to read this word.

MODEL **I see that the first vowel sound in this word is followed by two consonants. I will divide the word into syllables between them. I see the letters *oy* in the second syllable. I know these letters often stand for the /oi/ sound. I also see the ending *-ed*. I can blend the parts together to say this word.**

Guided Practice

Have students apply syllabication rules. Point out that students can apply syllabication rules whenever they read. Display Transparency 9 and have students apply what they have learned about syllabication to read the underlined words. When students come to the word *content*, remind them about the exception to the first-syllable accent rule.

Summarize. Ask students to explain how breaking words into syllables helps them read unfamiliar words.

SYLLABICATION

Have you ever seen a wild animal carrying its baby in a backpack? You might see that in a cartoon, but not in real life.

Animals have their own methods, or ways, to carry their young. They don't need extra equipment.

A kangaroo has a built-in pocket to carry its young. As the mother kangaroo hops around, the joey, or baby kangaroo, is content cuddled up inside its mother's pouch. Sometimes it will come out and hop around. If it senses danger, it hops right back in.

Crocodile babies get to ride in their mother's jaws while scorpions transport their young on their backs. Adult tigers use their teeth to pick their babies up by the scruff, or back, of their necks. The cub relaxes, and it doesn't hurt.

▲ Teaching Transparency 9

Practice/Apply

WORD HUNT

PERFORMANCE ASSESSMENT Organize students into small groups. Provide each group with an article from a wildlife magazine at the appropriate reading level. Ask students to list all the long unfamiliar words they find in the article. Have them work together to divide the words into syllables. Then have students share their lists and tell how to pronounce each word. List on the board words that students could not decode, and have the whole class work together to say these words. READING/WRITING

SYLLABLE PUZZLE

Have students draw circles and squares on a piece of paper. Then have them write in each shape one long word from the story or from the nature article. Have them create a puzzle by cutting out the shapes and then cutting the words into syllables. Students can exchange their puzzles, put them together, and read the words. READING/WRITING

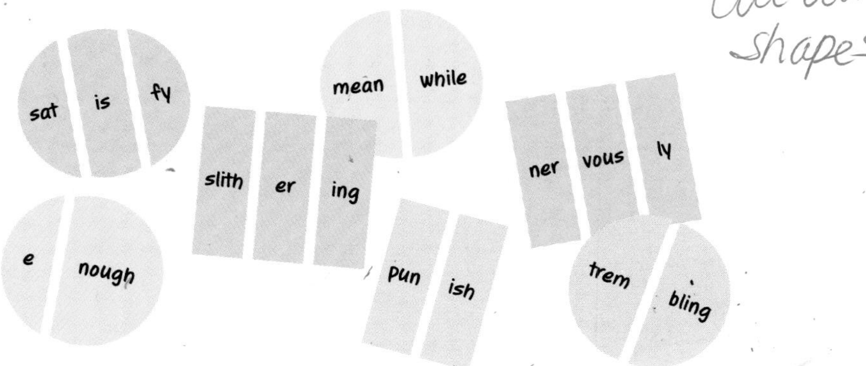

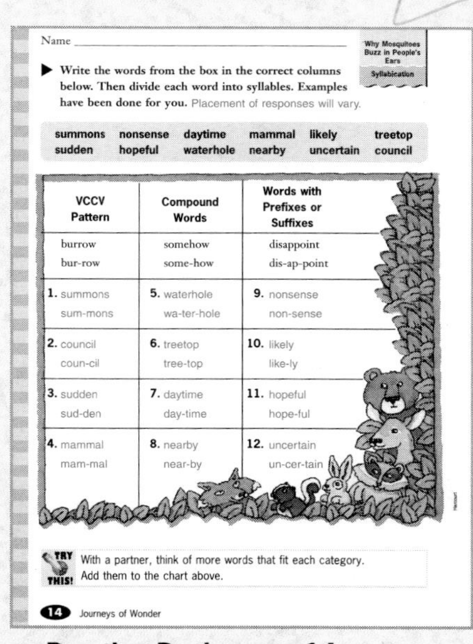

Name ____________

Why Mosquitoes Buzz in People's Ears
Syllabication

▶ Write the words from the box in the correct columns below. Then divide each word into syllables. Examples have been done for you. Placement of responses will vary.

summons nonsense daytime mammal likely treetop
sudden hopeful waterhole nearby uncertain council

VCCV Pattern	Compound Words	Words with Prefixes or Suffixes
burrow bur-row	somehow some-how	disappoint dis-ap-point
1. summons sum-mons	5. waterhole wa-ter-hole	9. nonsense non-sense
2. council coun-cil	6. treetop tree-top	10. likely like-ly
3. sudden sud-den	7. daytime day-time	11. hopeful hope-ful
4. mammal mam-mal	8. nearby near-by	12. uncertain un-cer-tain

TRY THIS! With a partner, think of more words that fit each category. Add them to the chart above.

14 Journeys of Wonder

▲ Practice Book, page 14

Vocabulary Workshop

Have students read the TAKE-HOME BOOK ***The World Next Door*** to reinforce vocabulary words. See also *Guided Reading Manual for Take-Home Books,* page 18.

Reviewing Vocabulary Words

Have students check the predict-o-grams they completed earlier. They should revise their predict-o-grams if necessary.

Predict-o-Gram		
Characters	**Setting**	**Events**
grumbling duty satisfied	council	nonsense mischief summons

Discuss with students how they know whether they have placed the vocabulary words in the right columns.

Have students work in pairs, each choosing a few vocabulary words and making lists of synonyms for each word. Students can make an index card for each vocabulary word they choose, writing the word on the front of the card and its synonyms on the back.

Students should practice reading irregular and regular words quickly and automatically by playing "Flash Fast" in pairs. One student should hold up cards one at a time as the other reads the word aloud.

Reviewing Word Identification Strategies

Use word order and context to confirm meaning. Ask students to reread pages 37–39, using word order and context to figure out the meaning of the following words: *lumbered, burrow, alarm, tidbit, dawn.* They can create a chart like the one below that lists each word and the context that helped them determine the meanings.

Word	Context
lumbered burrow	"pass by" "rabbit hole"

Cross-Curricular Words Encourage students to look through their social studies textbooks to find unfamiliar words. Tell them to use what they have learned about context and word order to figure out how to say the words and what they mean. (Possible words: *earthquake, government, nationality, telegraph, department, freedom, plantation, explorer, taxation*) Call on volunteers to read their words and tell how they used context to figure them out.

Extending Vocabulary

LISTING SOUND WORDS

Onomatopoeia In "Why Mosquitoes Buzz in People's Ears," the crow flies into the forest crying *kaa, kaa, kaa*. Explain to students that using words like *kaa* that name or imitate sounds is called **onomatopoeia**. Invite students to say the word *kaa*, making their voices sound like a crow's. Then help students develop a list of animals and their sounds.

Animal
Sound Word
crow
kaa
python/snake
hiss
owl
hoot
monkey
screech
lion
roar
mosquito
buzz

Place words in the list. You might begin by having students suggest names of animals in the story. Help students read the list, encouraging them to pronounce each word like the sound it imitates. Have students add other unusual animals and sound words to the list. (Possible responses: coyote/howl; parrot/squawk; seal/bark; donkey/bray)

ANIMALS OF AFRICA

Reference Sources/Encyclopedia Remind students that "Why Mosquitoes Buzz in People's Ears" is a West African folktale. Encourage them to use an encyclopedia to research the animals of Africa. Ask them to find information about one animal that is not mentioned in the story and to write the name of the animal and one or two interesting facts about it on a note card. Students can also draw a picture of the animal on the card. Suggest that students collect the cards, alphabetize them, and put them in a file box to use at the research station.

CHALLENGE

Students can make sound word lists for other categories, such as musical instruments. (Possible responses: drum/thump, thump; cymbals/clash; piano/plink) Students may enjoy using their lists of sound words to dramatize this story or another folktale, fairy tale, or nursery rhyme.

Name ________

Why Mosquitoes Buzz in People's Ears
Onomatopoeia

▶ On the lines, write two words from the box for the sounds each animal makes.

purr	caw	whinny	bark
tweet	woof	meow	neigh

1. woof
2. bark
3. purr
4. meow
5. tweet
6. caw
7. whinny
8. neigh

TRY THIS! Write and illustrate a story about a group of animals. In your story, use animal sounds.

Journeys of Wonder 15

▲ **Practice Book, page 15**

Informative Writing

PARAGRAPH THAT CONTRASTS

Connect Writing to Reading

Remind students that in "Why Mosquitoes Buzz in People's Ears" the trouble starts when the mosquito says something ridiculous to the iguana. The mosquito compares himself to a yam. Ask students whether they think a mosquito and a yam are similar or different. (different) Explain that writing that contrasts shows how people, places, or things are different.

Teach/Model

Display Transparency 10. Explain that a paragraph that contrasts may be organized the same way as a paragraph that compares.

STUDENT MODEL: PARAGRAPH THAT CONTRASTS

In a paragraph that contrasts, a writer shows how people, places, or things are different. Here is a paragraph that contrasts. It is part of a letter a student wrote to a cousin who is coming to visit for a weekend.

topic sentence	You'll see right away that the two dogs in my family are very different.
examples of differences	First, the dogs are not the same age. Mike is five years younger than Coco. Next, you'll notice that the dogs like to play in different ways. Mike likes to run and fetch a ball. Coco would rather lie around and chew on his leather bone. Last, the dogs have different sleeping habits. Mike hops up on the bed and sleeps next to me. Coco likes to curl up in a big basket.
main point restated	You'll never meet two dogs that are so different.

▲ Teaching Transparency 10

ANALYZE THE MODEL

- Audience—a cousin
- Writer's task—to show how the family's two dogs are different
- Differences writer gives—age, ways of playing, sleeping habits

FOCUS ON ORGANIZATION

- Main point stated in first sentence
- Differences presented in a logical order
- Order words used to separate the differences *(First, Next, Last)*
- Main point restated in different words at end

FOCUS ON ELABORATION

- Details develop each difference. (younger—older; plays ball—chews leather bone; sleeps on bed—sleeps in basket)
- Specific, vivid action words *(run and fetch, lie around, chew on, hop up, curl up)* develop the differences.

Writing Prompts

Choose one of the following:

A Assign a prompt, for example:
Write a letter to a friend that contrasts two people you know. The two people might be yourself and another person. Give examples of how the two people are different. Put your examples in a logical order.

B Have students write a paragraph that contrasts two places or things of their own choosing.

TECHNOLOGY

Students can use a word processing program such as *ClarisWorks for Kids®* to plan and write their paragraphs that contrast.

Prewrite and Draft

Have students choose a subject and brainstorm qualities they could contrast—for example, age, appearance, personality, interests. When they decide which qualities they want to focus on, they may use a graphic organizer like the one on Transparency 11 to record their thoughts.

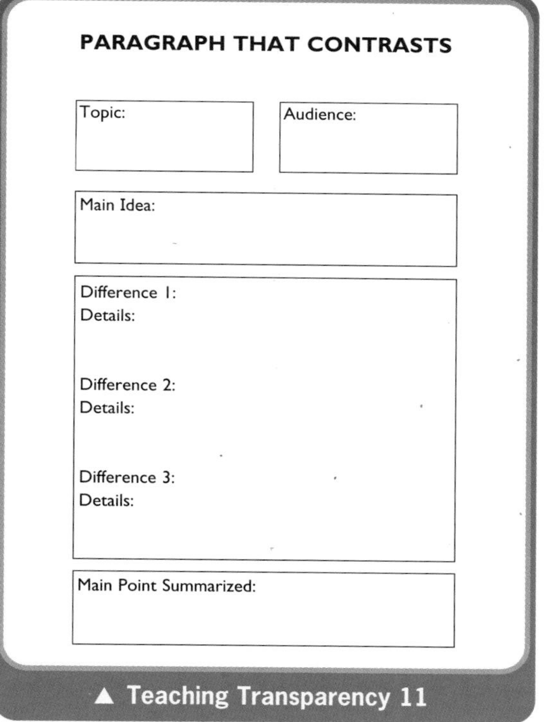

PARAGRAPH THAT CONTRASTS
Topic:
Audience:
Main Idea:
Difference 1:
Details:
Difference 2:
Details:
Difference 3:
Details:
Main Point Summarized:

▲ Teaching Transparency 11

Revise

Have students work in pairs or small groups to discuss their paragraphs that contrast. To help students work together constructively, provide the following questions:

- **Does the topic sentence clearly state what is being contrasted?**
- **Do you give several differences that support your topic sentence?**
- **Do you give details that add information about the differences you mention?**
- **Are the differences in a logical order?**
- **Does the last sentence summarize the point of the contrast?**

After students have discussed each other's writing, have them revise their own paragraphs that contrast.

SCORING RUBRIC FOR SUGGESTED PROMPT

4 Advanced At the beginning, the writer clearly states what qualities will be contrasted. At least three differences support the main idea and are presented in a logical order. Details develop the differences. The letter restates the main idea at the end. The writer uses language the friend would enjoy.

3 Proficient The writer states a main idea in a topic sentence at the beginning. At least three differences support the idea, and they are fairly well organized. However, few details elaborate on the differences. The last sentence restates the main idea. The language is appropriate for a letter to a friend.

2 Basic The writer states a main idea in a topic sentence. Only one or two examples of differences support the main idea. The transition from one difference to the next is not clear. The writer offers few, if any, details. The ending restates the main idea. The language is generally appropriate for a letter to a friend.

1 Below Basic The writer has not clearly stated the main idea in a topic sentence, and the paragraph contains few supporting details. The differences are not presented in a logical order. The writer forgets the audience and does not use language that makes the differences clear.

Assessment

STUDENT SELF- AND PEER-ASSESSMENT

Give students copies of the four-point scoring rubric, page R84, and have them suggest other important points. They may use the rubric to evaluate their own and/or each other's paragraphs that contrast.

PORTFOLIO OPPORTUNITY

Students may keep their revised pieces in their work portfolios and complete their pieces later.

Test Prep

Remind students that during writing tests they should

- make prewriting notes or graphic organizers.
- use words that make clear when they are going from one point of contrast to the next.
- keep their audience in mind.

INFORMATIVE WRITING—CLASSIFICATION

Additional lessons:
Paragraph That Compares T44
Paragraph That Classifies T136
Complete Writing Process: T180
Tested or Timed Writing: T226

Language Handbook, page 54

GRAMMAR

Adjectives for *What Kind*

SKILL TRACE	
INTRODUCE	T98–T99
Review	T117

Language Handbook, pages 120–121

REACHING ALL LEARNERS

ESL

Review color and shape words with students. Display attribute blocks, and have students describe their colors and shapes.

DAY 1 Teach/Model

DAILY LANGUAGE PRACTICE

1. **Suppose the sun did not rise one day?** (day.)
2. **i could never imagine such a thinge.** (I; thing)

INTRODUCE THE CONCEPT Remind students that an adjective is a word that describes a noun. Display sentences 1–3 and the charts on Transparency 12 and discuss these points:

- Some adjectives tell *what kind.*
- Adjectives that tell what kind can describe size, shape, or color.
- Adjectives that tell what kind can tell how something looks, sounds, feels, tastes, or smells.

Have volunteers read each chart column aloud and list two additional examples for each column. (Responses will vary.)

ADJECTIVES FOR *WHAT KIND*

1. A mosquito bit me.
2. A tiny mosquito bit me.
3. A noisy mosquito bit me.

ADJECTIVES FOR SIZE, SHAPE, AND COLOR

Size	Shape	Color
huge	round	blue
tiny	oblong	silvery
skinny	square	orange

ADJECTIVES FOR THE SENSES

Sight	Sound	Touch	Taste	Smell
colorful	noisy	fuzzy	delicious	sweet
pretty	buzzing	smooth	spicy	rotten
dark	quiet	sticky	minty	stinky

▲ Teaching Transparency 12

DAY 2 Extend the Concept

DAILY LANGUAGE PRACTICE

1. **Oure class read a story. About the sunn.** (Our; story about; sun)
2. **the story comes from africa.** (The; Africa)

BUILD ORAL LANGUAGE Give students the list of animals below and have them develop oral sentences that describe each animal's size, shape, color, and feel.

iguana	rabbit
snake	owl

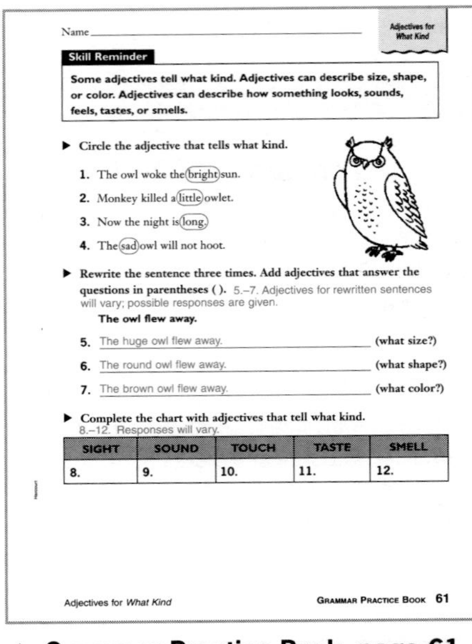

Name ____________ Adjectives for What Kind

Skill Reminder

Some adjectives tell what kind. Adjectives can describe size, shape, or color. Adjectives can describe how something looks, sounds, feels, tastes, or smells.

▶ **Circle the adjective that tells what kind.**

1. The owl woke the (bright) sun.
2. Monkey killed a (little) owlet.
3. Now the night is (long.)
4. The (sad) owl will not hoot.

▶ **Rewrite the sentence three times. Add adjectives that answer the questions in parentheses ( ).** 5.–7. Adjectives for rewritten sentences will vary; possible responses are given.

The owl flew away.

5. The huge owl flew away. (what size?)
6. The round owl flew away. (what shape?)
7. The brown owl flew away. (what color?)

▶ **Complete the chart with adjectives that tell what kind.** 8.–12. Responses will vary.

SIGHT	SOUND	TOUCH	TASTE	SMELL
8.	9.	10.	11.	12.

Adjectives for *What Kind* GRAMMAR PRACTICE BOOK 61

▲ Grammar Practice Book, page 61

DAY 3 Oral Review/Practice

DAILY LANGUAGE PRACTICE

1. **Meny storys are about animals.** (Many stories)
2. **Sometimes our teacher reads stores to we.** (stories; us)

SIZE, SHAPE, AND COLOR Write these sentences on the board:

The ________ rabbit scurried.

The snake was ________.

Then make a chart with the headings *Size, Shape, Color.* Have volunteers suggest adjectives that could complete each sentence with details of size, shape, or color. Write the adjectives in the chart as they are mentioned.

Name ________

Adjectives for What Kind

▶ Look at the pictures. Place each adjective in the correct column.

tiny curved black spotted slender
long large pointed patterned

	SIZE	SHAPE	COLOR
	1. tiny	4. pointed	7. spotted
	2. large	5. curved	8. black
	3. long	6. slender	9. patterned

▶ Choose one picture from those above. Write three sentences that describe it. Use the adjectives you wrote in the boxes.
Sentences will vary.

10. ________
11. ________
12. ________

62 GRAMMAR PRACTICE BOOK — Adjectives for *What Kind*

▲ Grammar Practice Book, page 62

DAY 4 Apply to Writing

DAILY LANGUAGE PRACTICE

1. **in this story. A little mosquito makes a big mistake.** (In this story a)
2. **the owl must hoot each daye to wake the sun.** (The; day)

DESCRIBING A PICTURE Have students write a description of a picture from the story. Ask them to use adjectives that tell about size, shape, and color as well as any other adjectives that describe the picture clearly. Students should circle any adjectives they use.

> **Test Prep**
>
> Share with students these tips about identifying and using adjectives.
>
> - Adjectives may tell about a noun's size, shape, or color.
> - Adjectives may appeal to the sense of sight, hearing, touch, taste, or smell.

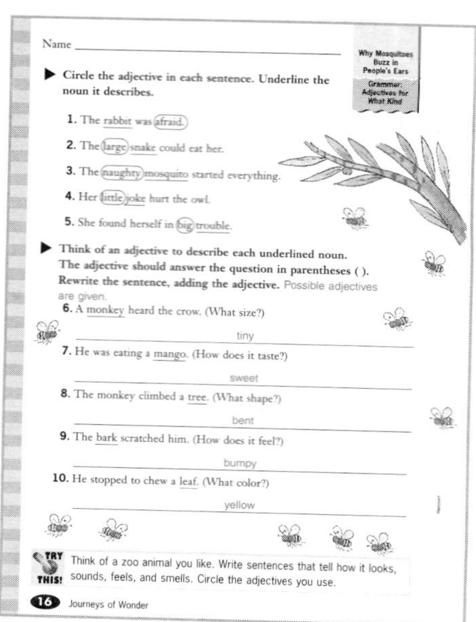

Name ________

Why Mosquitoes Buzz in People's Ears — Grammar: Adjectives for What Kind

▶ Circle the adjective in each sentence. Underline the noun it describes.

1. The rabbit was afraid.
2. The large snake could eat her.
3. The naughty mosquito started everything.
4. Her little joke hurt the owl.
5. She found herself in big trouble.

▶ Think of an adjective to describe each underlined noun. The adjective should answer the question in parentheses ( ). Rewrite the sentence, adding the adjective. Possible adjectives are given.

6. A monkey heard the crow. (What size?) tiny
7. He was eating a mango. (How does it taste?) sweet
8. The monkey climbed a tree. (What shape?) bent
9. The bark scratched him. (How does it feel?) bumpy
10. He stopped to chew a leaf. (What color?) yellow

TRY THIS! Think of a zoo animal you like. Write sentences that tell how it looks, sounds, feels, and smells. Circle the adjectives you use.

16 Journeys of Wonder

▲ Practice Book, page 16

DAY 5 Cumulative Review

DAILY LANGUAGE PRACTICE

1. **The king calls a meeting. Because Mother Owl does not hoot?** (meeting because; hoot.)
2. **He lerns that Mother Owl is to sad to hoot.** (learns; too sad)

NOUNS AND ADJECTIVES Have students copy the sentences below, circling the adjectives and underlining the noun each adjective describes.

1. The iguana was (grumpy).
2. A (foolish) mosquito annoyed him.
3. The mosquito told a (silly) story.

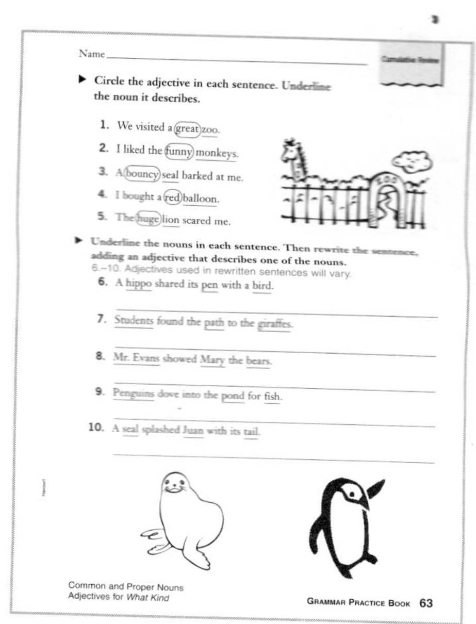

Name ________

Cumulative Review

▶ Circle the adjective in each sentence. Underline the noun it describes.

1. We visited a great zoo.
2. I liked the funny monkeys.
3. A bouncy seal barked at me.
4. I bought a red balloon.
5. The huge lion scared me.

▶ Underline the nouns in each sentence. Then rewrite the sentence, adding an adjective that describes one of the nouns.
6.–10. Adjectives used in rewritten sentences will vary.

6. A hippo shared its pen with a bird.
7. Students found the path to the giraffes.
8. Mr. Evans showed Mary the bears.
9. Penguins dove into the pond for fish.
10. A seal splashed Juan with its tail.

Common and Proper Nouns
Adjectives for *What Kind* — GRAMMAR PRACTICE BOOK 63

▲ Grammar Practice Book, page 63

SPELLING

Homophones

SPELLING WORDS

1. one*
2. won
3. hour
4. way*
5. heard*
6. flower
7. our
8. flour
9. weigh
10. herd

BONUS WORDS

11. weather
12. whether

*Words appearing in "Why Mosquitoes Buzz in People's Ears." Additional story words following the generalization are *would (wood), two, too (to), through (threw), hole (whole), not (knot), night (knight), sun (son), bear (bare), hear (here), break (brake).*

STUDENT-CHOSEN WORDS

13. ______
14. ______
15. ______

INTERVENTION

Invite less-proficient spellers to add easier Student-Chosen Words that follow the generalizations—such as *sun-son* or *two-to* —to their weekly lists.

DAY 1 Pretest/Self-Check

ADMINISTER THE PRETEST. Say each word, and then use it in a Dictation Sentence. (See Day 5.) Help students self-check their pretests using the list at the top of Transparency 13.

OPEN SORT Have students look for ways to sort the Spelling Words. For example, they might sort them according to parts of speech or beginning letters. Ask volunteers to share their categories and sorted lists.

Words Beginning with h
hour
heard
herd

HOMOPHONES

Spelling Words

1. one	6. flower
2. won	7. our
3. hour	8. flour
4. way	9. weigh
5. heard	10. herd

Words That Sound Alike in Pairs

Homophone Pairs	
one	won
way	weigh
flower	flour
heard	herd
hour	our

Homophones are pairs of words that sound the same but have different spellings and meanings.

▲ Teaching Transparency 13

DAY 2 Teach/Model

CLOSED SORT Display Transparency 13, or write the information on the board. Ask students to write each homophone pair where it belongs.

Point to and read the words *one* and *won*. Ask students what is the same and different about these two words. (They sound the same; they are spelled differently; they have different meanings.) Have students read the generalization to confirm their conclusion.

Handwriting Tip

Remind students that each letter they write should be the correct size. Tall letters touch both the top and bottom lines.

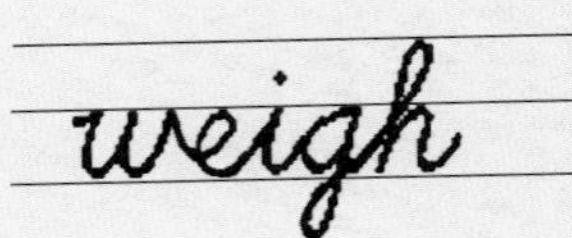

Name ______ Why Mosquitoes Buzz in People's Ears Homophones

▶ Write the Spelling Words from the box to complete the sentences.

our heard weigh herd way hour

"Have you **(1)** heard about the **(2)** herd of animals that trampled over our field last week?" asked Barry. "They ran all the **(3)** way down to the river. Can you imagine what all those animals must **(4)** weigh? In just about an **(5)** hour, they changed the look of **(6)** our field."

▶ Write a Spelling Word from the box to match each picture.

one won flower flour

7. flower
8. won
9. flour
10. one

Handwriting Tip: Loop an *e* so it doesn't look like an *i*. Write these words.

e

11. heard ______
12. weigh ______

SCHOOL-HOME CONNECTION With your child, make up sentences that use pairs of homophones. Here are a few examples: Add the prices in that ad. I'll be walking down the aisle.

Journeys of Wonder 17

▲ Practice Book, page 17

DAY 3 Spelling Strategies

LOOK FOR HOMOPHONES Write the following sentences on the board:

I picked a flour from the garden.

I need flower to make a cake.

Read both sentences and ask students which words sound the same in both sentences. Have volunteers circle those words. Then ask: Do the words *flour* and *flower* make sense in the sentences? Suggest that students give a definition of each word so they can see that the words as spelled should be switched in the sentences. Repeat this activity with other homophones from the spelling list.

Apply to Writing

Have students look for homophones in their writing and check to make sure that each word they've written is spelled correctly to make sense in the sentence.

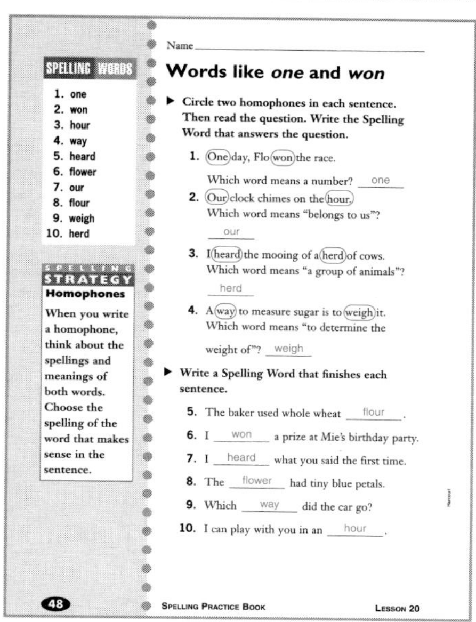

Name ____________

SPELLING WORDS

1. one
2. won
3. hour
4. way
5. heard
6. flower
7. our
8. flour
9. weigh
10. herd

SPELLING STRATEGY

Homophones

When you write a homophone, think about the spellings and meanings of both words. Choose the spelling of the word that makes sense in the sentence.

Words like *one* and *won*

▶ **Circle two homophones in each sentence. Then read the question. Write the Spelling Word that answers the question.**

1. One day, Flo won the race. Which word means a number? one
2. Our clock chimes on the hour. Which word means "belongs to us"? our
3. I heard the mooing of a herd of cows. Which word means "a group of animals"? herd
4. A way to measure sugar is to weigh it. Which word means "to determine the weight of"? weigh

▶ **Write a Spelling Word that finishes each sentence.**

5. The baker used whole wheat flour.
6. I won a prize at Mie's birthday party.
7. I heard what you said the first time.
8. The flower had tiny blue petals.
9. Which way did the car go?
10. I can play with you in an hour.

48 Spelling Practice Book Lesson 20

▲ **Spelling Practice Book, page 48**

DAY 4 Spelling Activities

HOMOPHONE PAIRS Create a list of homophones written in two columns in mixed-up order. Make several copies of the list. Have pairs of students take turns drawing a line between two words that are homophones. Here is an example:

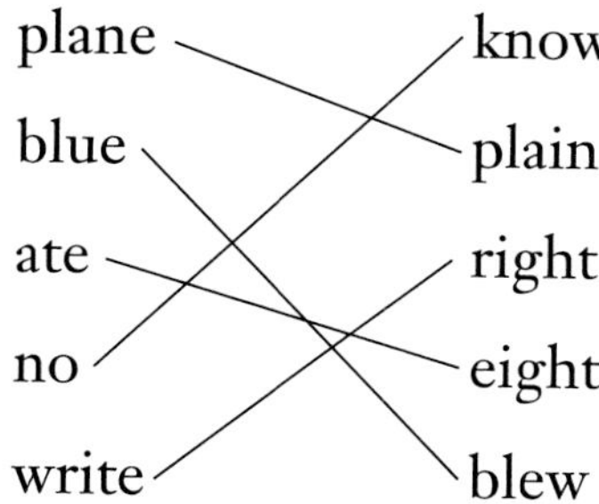

HOMOPHONE SENTENCES Challenge students to use their Spelling and Bonus Words to write sentences, using a homophone pair in each sentence. Have them share their sentences with a partner.

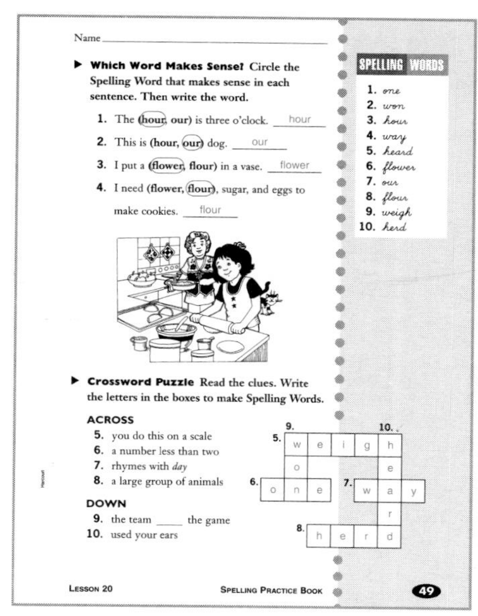

Name ____________

▶ **Which Word Makes Sense?** Circle the Spelling Word that makes sense in each sentence. Then write the word.

1. The (hour, our) is three o'clock. hour
2. This is (hour, our) dog. our
3. I put a (flower, flour) in a vase. flower
4. I need (flower, flour), sugar, and eggs to make cookies. flour

▶ **Crossword Puzzle** Read the clues. Write the letters in the boxes to make Spelling Words.

ACROSS
5. you do this on a scale
6. a number less than two
7. rhymes with *day*
8. a large group of animals

DOWN
9. the team ____ the game
10. used your ears

SPELLING WORDS

1. one
2. won
3. hour
4. way
5. heard
6. flower
7. our
8. flour
9. weigh
10. herd

Lesson 20 Spelling Practice Book 49

▲ **Spelling Practice Book, page 49**

DAY 5 Posttest

Assess students' progress using the Dictation Sentences.

DICTATION SENTENCES

1. **one** Only one child got all the answers right on the math quiz.
2. **won** She won first prize for her science project.
3. **hour** In one hour school will be out for the day.
4. **way** I was a long way from home when I hurt my knee.
5. **heard** Dad heard the neighbors' dog barking all night long.
6. **flower** This flower has at least fifty petals.
7. **our** Our grandparents live in Ohio.
8. **flour** Flour is needed to make bread, cookies, and cakes.
9. **weigh** I will step on the scale to find how much I weigh.
10. **herd** A herd of cattle grazed near the stream.

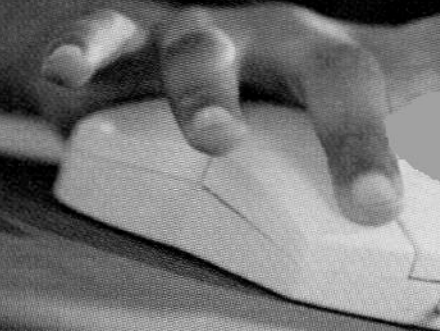

Cross-Curricular Connections

MULTI-AGE CLASSROOMS

Encourage the development of leadership skills in older students by having them guide the research phase of the Exploring the Serengeti activity. Remind them to assign a task to everyone in the group, including the younger students, without being bossy or impolite.

ESL

Students with strong artistic talents but limited proficiency in writing and communication skills can be assigned the role of art director for the poster portion of the Exploring the Serengeti activity.

INTERNET Related cross-curricular resources can be found on *The Learning Site* at **www.harcourtschool.com**

SCIENCE

Exploring the Serengeti

MATERIALS

- computer with Internet access
- encyclopedia
- paper
- pencils
- crayons and markers
- old wildlife magazines to cut up (optional)

RESEARCH ANIMAL BEHAVIOR AND THE SERENGETI The art and the text of "Why Mosquitoes Buzz in People's Ears" show the diversity of animal life in Africa. The story also provides clues to the natural habitats, or living places, of these animals and shows how the animals interact and depend on each other for survival. Encourage students to learn more about animal behavior and interaction by using an encyclopedia, science magazines, and the Internet to research the Serengeti.

Explain to students that the Serengeti is an area in Africa where millions of wild animals live. Have small groups research the ecosystem of the Serengeti. Students can use what they learn to create posters with pictures of the animals.

Activity Card 34, page R14, will help students focus their research and create their posters. They should then use the posters as visual aids to clarify and support brief oral reports to the class.

FOCUS SKILL After students do their research, have them discuss how syllabication helped them identify and understand long words related to the topic.

VIEWING/READING ELECTRONIC TEXTS/INQUIRY/ART

► Exploring the Serengeti — ACTIVITY CARD 34

In "Why Mosquitoes Buzz in People's Ears," the animals of the forest depend on the crow to spread the alarm in case of danger. In real life, wild animals also depend on each other to survive. This is how an ecosystem works.

Do research on the Internet to learn about the ecosystem of the Serengeti in Africa. Type the word *Serengeti* in the search box. Then search the results for answers to these questions:

- Where is the Serengeti? What does it look like? What is the weather like?
- What special features do some animals have that help them survive there?
- How do the animals protect themselves?
- What threats are there to the animals' survival?

Make a poster that shows in pictures and words how the ecosystem of the Serengeti works.

▲ Activity Card 34

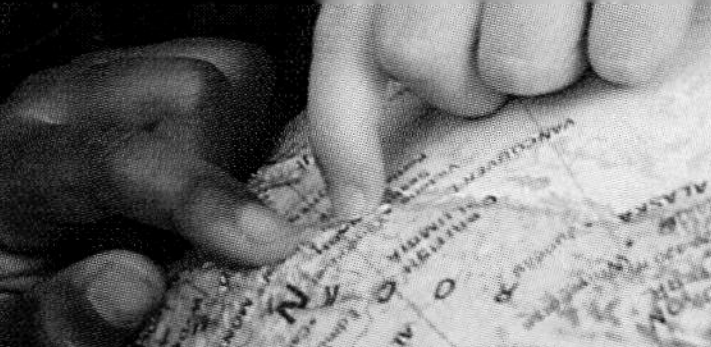
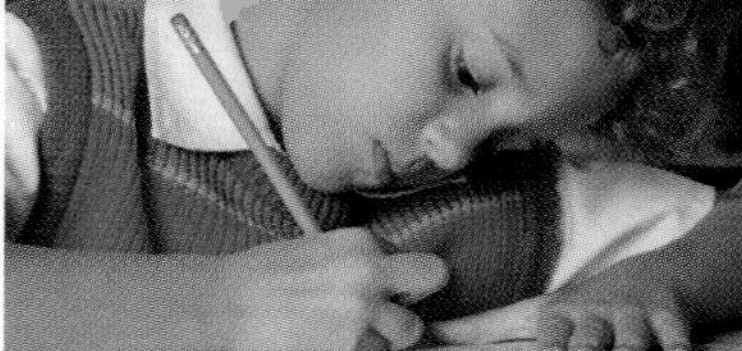

MUSIC

Sounds of the Forest

MATERIALS
- tape recorder
- cassette
- traditional African music

WRITE A SONG In "Why Mosquitoes Buzz in People's Ears," the repetition of words and sounds lends a musical quality to the text and helps create an awareness of the many sounds of a forest or jungle. These are the sounds of nature, the sounds that often inspire the music of a land and its people. Have students listen to recordings of traditional African music to pick out sounds that might have been inspired by the sounds of nature. Then students can write their own song that retells this folktale or another one they know.

Encourage groups of students to

- decide on a tune for their song before they write the words.
- look through the story to find nature sounds and words to use in the lyrics, or for background sounds for their song: for example, *badamin*, *wasawusu*, *krik*, *kaa*, and *so sad*.
- practice and record their song.

Provide an opportunity for students to share their songs with the class. MUSIC/WRITING

RESEARCH

Inquiry Projects

"Why Mosquitoes Buzz in People's Ears" can be a springboard for inquiry into a variety of topics and ideas. Brainstorm topics students would like to learn more about, and write their ideas in a web. Students can use some resources shown here to begin their inquiry projects.

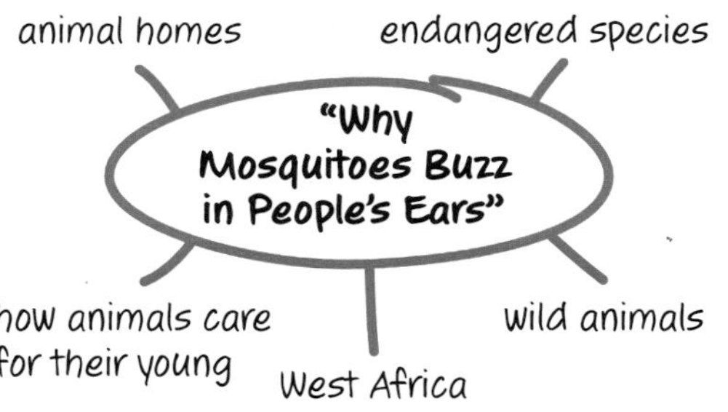

RESOURCES

How the Ostrich Got Its Long Neck by Verna Aardema. Scholastic, 1995.

Anansi Finds a Fool by Verna Aardema. Dial, 1992. AVERAGE

READER'S CHOICE LIBRARY
The Wave by Margaret Hodges. AVERAGE

Bugs and Other Insects by Bobbie Kalman and Tammy Everts. Crabtree, 1994. CHALLENGING

"A Bookworm Who

THEME
Tell Me a Story

GENRE:
Autobiography

- A **biographical** story that is told in the **first person**.
- Events are usually in **time order**.
- The writer expresses **personal thoughts** and **feelings**.

CROSS-CURRICULAR CONNECTIONS

- **SOCIAL STUDIES:** Compare Two Regions
- **SCIENCE/ART:** Swamp Community Mural

FOCUS STRATEGY SUMMARIZE

- **Before Reading:** Strategy Reminder on page T113
- **During Reading:** Apply the Strategy on page T120

FOCUS SKILL FACT AND OPINION

- **Before Reading:** Introduce the Skill on pages T112–T113
- **During Reading:** Apply the Skill on pages T116, T118, T122
- **After Reading:** Practice the Skill on pages T130–T131 (*Student Edition* 74–75)

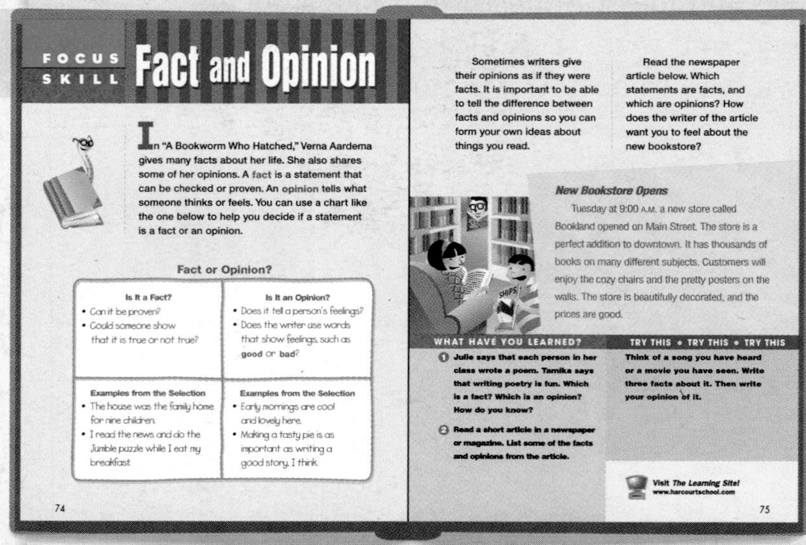

FOCUS SKILL **Fact and Opinion**

In "A Bookworm Who Hatched," Verna Aardema gives many facts about her life. She also shares some of her opinions. A fact is a statement that can be checked or proven. An opinion tells what someone thinks or feels. You can use a chart like the one below to help you decide if a statement is a fact or an opinion.

Fact or Opinion?

Is It a Fact?	Is It an Opinion?
• Can it be proven? • Could someone show that it is true or not true?	• Does it tell a person's feelings? • Does the writer use words that show feelings, such as **good** or **bad**?
Examples from the Selection • The house was the family home for nine children. • I read the news and do the Jumble puzzle while I eat my breakfast.	**Examples from the Selection** • Early mornings are cool and lovely here. • Making a tasty pie is as important as writing a good story, I think.

74

Sometimes writers give their opinions as if they were facts. It is important to be able to tell the difference between facts and opinions so you can form your own ideas about things you read.

Read the newspaper article below. Which statements are facts, and which are opinions? How does the writer of the article want you to feel about the new bookstore?

New Bookstore Opens

Tuesday at 9:00 A.M. a new store called Bookland opened on Main Street. The store is a perfect addition to downtown. It has thousands of books on many different subjects. Customers will enjoy the cozy chairs and the pretty posters on the walls. The store is beautifully decorated, and the prices are good.

WHAT HAVE YOU LEARNED?

1. **Julie says that each person in her class wrote a poem. Tamika says that writing poetry is fun. Which is a fact? Which is an opinion? How do you know?**
2. **Read a short article in a newspaper or magazine. List some of the facts and opinions from the article.**

TRY THIS • TRY THIS • TRY THIS

Think of a song you have heard or a movie you have seen. Write three facts about it. Then write your opinion of it.

Visit *The Learning Site!* www.harcourtschool.com

75

▲ **Student Edition, pages 74–75**